My
Naked
Journey

My Naked Journey

A Reiki Master's Quest to Live Authentically

Maureen O'Shaughnessy

PUA'ENA PUBLISHING
KAILUA, HAWAII

Published by Pua'ena Publishing
PMB 732 150 Hamakua Drive
Kailua, Hawaii 96734
reiki@hawaii.rr.com
www.reiki-hawaii.com

Publisher Cataloging-in-Publication (PCIP) Data
O'Shaughnessy, Maureen.
    My naked journey : a Reiki master's quest to live authentically
/ Maureen O'Shaughnessy. —Kailua, HI: Pua'ena Publishing, 2003.
        p.   cm.
    ISBN   0-9722491-0-9

Includes bibliographical references.

    1. O'Shaughnessy, Maureen. 2. Reiki (Healing system). 3. Mind
    and body. 4. Mental healing. 5. Alternative medicine. I. Title.

RZ403.R45 085   2003   2002111338
615.851—dc21   CIP
07 06 05 04 03 ◆ 5 4 3 2 1

Printed in the United States of America

Project coordinated by To The Point Solutions
zazattc@traverse.net

COVER ART: Pastel painting (without footprints), by Barbara J. Roman,
808-262-4708, broman882@aol.com, RomanArtStudios.com
FOOTPRINTS digitally added by Jerry Fujioka, Honolulu, HI
COVER AND TEXT DESIGN: Mary Jo Zazueta
AUTHOR PHOTOS: Terri L. Alexander, Honolulu, HI

This book is dedicated to all of my Reiki students—who have honored me with their trust in choosing me to initiate them into the wonder of Reiki.

And especially to those of you who have read my newsletters over the past seven years, shared my stories with others, and have let me know that what I wrote mattered to you. This book would not have happened without you.

Mahalo, Maureen

Contents

Contents

Acknowledgments

This book would not have come about without the encouragement and suggestions of the many people who have read my newsletter over the past few years.

I especially would like to acknowledge Dr. Anita Johnston, who has patiently steered me along my journey; and my initiating Reiki Master, Jessica Osborn-Turner, who provided me with this path.

Also all of my many friends who have listened to me, cried with me, laughed with (and sometimes at) me, and were honest with me. Some of you are: Roe Mulvihill, Suzanne Allen, Liza Delin, Dee Wescott, Agnes Foos, Lynn Eastman, Jerry Fujioka, Holly Lawrence, and Molly Elliot. The rest of you know who you are.

Thanks to Susan Henderson for the typing, Beth Terry for the help and advice, Jerry Fujioka for assistance with the cover, and Mary Jo Zazueta for keeping me on track and coordinating the process.

Introduction

Many of us impart on a journey without having any idea where it will ultimately take us. I was one of those people. I chose to become a Reiki Master because I loved how Reiki made me feel and I wanted more of it. (Sort of like chocolate!) I didn't have any dreams or visions of what becoming a Reiki Master would entail, and I didn't think it would change my life. I expected that I would continue in my corporate job and on occasional weekends I might teach Reiki to a few others; as one might practice a hobby, like music, painting, or ceramics. In truth, I had no idea where I was headed!

For those of you who are unfamiliar with Reiki, it is a specific practice of hands-on healing using the universal "life force energy" found in all living things. This practice was re-discovered in Japan in the early 1900s and has become widespread throughout the world during the past twenty years. Reiki speeds up healing, provides pain relief, and alleviates the symptoms of stress in our day-to-day lives.

A Reiki Master is someone who has had specific training to

initiate others into the practice of Reiki. (For more information on Reiki, see the Bibliography at the back of this book.)

Although my journey began when I chose to learn Reiki in 1991, I was not aware that I had embarked on a journey until 1994. That was when I committed to my yearlong training with Jessica Osborn-Turner, my Reiki Master, to become a Reiki Master myself.

It was as if I had stepped onto a boat to enjoy the view and the sensation of floating on water. I had been drifting gently for a couple of years, smelling the salt air and enjoying the deep turquoise of the Hawaiian sea—without realizing that the boat had left the shore.

In 1994, after committing to this deeper relationship with Reiki (and therefore, myself), I suddenly hit the surf! My life turned upside down in a matter of weeks. Capsized, you could say. I quit my job, sold my car, my furniture, and most of my belongings. I gave up the lease on my house and had no idea what I was going to do. Needless to say, my family and friends were somewhat concerned!

The amazing thing was that this was simply the external, visible part of my journey. In September of 1995 I completed my training and was initiated as a Reiki Master. The storm calmed and I climbed back onto my boat. The scenery was still beautiful; the sun was shining yet I had no idea who I truly was. I was adrift with no land in sight and wasn't sure where the current would take me.

I started teaching Reiki classes and began to send out a newsletter. In the newsletter I wrote a column about Reiki. Gradually, the column changed and became a place where I shared different realizations about myself and my life "out loud"— inner issues that I was struggling with.

Many people commented on how courageous I was to share such vulnerable and personal information about myself with the general public ...for the world to see. I later realized that I was moved to do this for two reasons. The first reason was that I noticed many people made the assumption that since I was a Reiki Master I had "arrived," that I had it all together and they could look up to me. My ego liked this image a lot; however, the honest part of me knew how far from the truth this was. By sharing my vulnerabilities, faults, flaws, and struggles, people would see that being a Reiki Master did not make me even close to perfect. Instead, having Reiki in my life in a deeper way, was a catalyst that caused me to grow. It nourished me in a way that nurtured my inner growth, the infinite unfolding of the woman I am truly capable of becoming.

The second reason for "baring my soul" (hence, *My 'Naked' Journey*) was that I discovered that some of my deepest learning ... those great insights ... never came to me when I was alone, but always when I was sharing my thoughts with a friend. It was as if I needed someone else to hear my stories before I could own them or let them go.

Thus, over the past seven years, I wrote in my newsletter about the various issues that I struggled with in my life. I found that over time I became more honest with myself, clearer about what I valued, and I saw where there were often inconsistencies between what I thought I believed about myself and my world and how I behaved. People have consistently responded to what I wrote saying they were inspired and sometimes comforted to know someone else experienced the same things they did.

We often expect that a path or journey will take us some-where — a particular destination. I have discovered that this journey is lifelong and not linear. In fact, I see it spiraling upward where I greet the same issues over and over again, yet I have a slightly different perspective each time. Rather than expecting to finally arrive, I have come to welcome familiar scenery from a new angle and a new appreciation. I acknowledge the growth I have made and anticipate with excitement (rather than the dread and trepidation I often felt in the past) the new parts of me that I discover!

My purpose in publishing this book is to share my inner thoughts and insights with the hope that they will touch those of you who may be on a similar journey. I believe that there are many of us striving to live an honest, conscious, and authentic life. Perhaps my journey will inspire some of you to take this path also.

one

HONESTY

One of the reasons this book is titled My Naked Journey *is because I chose to be honest in what I wrote. It doesn't always make me look good, it sometimes can be uncomfortable, but if I am to "walk my talk" and live as I believe, then honesty is my only option.*

Some will debate that there are times and circumstances when honesty is not the best policy; that white lies can avoid hurting people's feelings (such as when a husband is asked by his wife if her new pants make her look fat!); or that there are times when someone doesn't need to know something and the truth would unnecessarily hurt them (such as when there was an affair, it's over and it won't happen again). I disagree.

If I am to live an authentic life, with sincere intimacy in my close relationships, then I believe I need to be truly honest ... all the time ... because ...

There Are No Secrets

One of the effects of Reiki training is that it strengthens our innate abilities—our creativity, our unique gifts, AND our intuition.

After taking the Reiki class many people find that their intuitive sense becomes stronger and clearer. In class we sometimes discuss how to deal with information we may intuitively perceive. When we discuss our intuitive perceptions it makes some people uncomfortable.

Everything about us is visible to others. All they need to do is look intuitively. Many times we are not conscious of the information we pick up, but we still respond to it.

The more I work with and teach Reiki, the more obvious it has become that there are no secrets. Everything I think, say, and do is available for others to know.

When we think a thought, speak, or take action, we create an energetic effect. This energy may be invisible, but it is very real! We can even measure the energy our thoughts produce with an EEG! We all respond to other's energy, whether we are aware of it or not. For example, we know when someone behind us is looking at us (don't we turn around to see who it is?) by feeling the flow of their *Ki* energy towards us. We also know what others are thinking, feeling, and doing. We just have to know how to pay attention to their energy, and they, in turn, will know the same about us!

Does that idea make you feel uncomfortable? How about when we judge someone we meet by their appearance? What if they really HEARD our thoughts? They do. They may not consciously say to themselves, "He thinks I'm a dumb blonde" but they will feel uncomfortable because they KNOW they have just been judged. We know it, too!

We live in a culture that perpetuates the myth that we can keep certain information from others "What they don't know won't hurt them." For example: spouses who have affairs, and the little things we don't discuss about ourselves because we are embarrassed about them. In fact, we live in a society where we are encouraged to lie. Think of the excuses we give when we turn down an invitation (we aren't busy, but say we are when we really just want some time for ourselves). Many people feel that President Clinton's dishonesty was justified or at least acceptable. "Everyone lies, especially politicians!" One person even commented to me that the public was responsible for Clinton's dishonesty, since they would have condemned him if he had told the truth!

Whether we hide information from others through lying or omission, we are fooling ourselves if we think they don't know! In fact, we are actually harming ourselves when we are dishonest or hiding things. If we could see the energy fields that emanate from us when we lie (and some people can!), we would see a CLASH. For example, if we hear a tone, and then another tone is played that is discordant and is not in harmony (or in sync) with the first tone, there is a clash of sound that actually hurts our ears. This discordance between our Truth and what we say or do creates an energetic clash that we all feel! (In my advanced Second Degree Workshop, we sometimes do an exercise where we are able to FEEL the difference in our bodies when we hear a true or a false statement.)

This clash in energy has a harmful affect on us. It disrupts our balance on all levels: physical, mental, emotional, and spiritual! If there is enough discordant energy within us, it can even manifest in illness! (Maybe the story of Pinocchio has more truth than we thought.) What if cancer is a result of energetic discordance in our bodies? Cancer is a disruption in the way our cells multiply and grow, so what if this energetic discordance interferes with the orderliness of our cell growth?

So, besides the fact that we aren't fooling anyone when we keep secrets or lie, we may even be harming ourselves!

Imagine what life would be like if we were completely open and told the truth all the time. How different would our lives be?

It's refreshing (and a relief) for me to admit that I am not perfect and to acknowledge when I feel insecure. When I tell the truth, people seem to be more accepting of me. Life becomes simpler and easier when I don't feel the need to pretend I am someone I am not.

I strive daily to be more open and honest. At times it becomes uncomfortable. When I remember that all that I think is not private or secret, I behave differently towards others. I stop my judgmental thoughts more quickly (I still have them, though!) and I can be more spontaneous . . . whatever I am thinking comes out of my mouth!

This honesty has also created some hurt, however. I once shared something I had done with a mutual acquaintance, which included another person. The person who participated in the event with me was very hurt and angry when they found out I had shared something that they felt was very private. I apologized and learned that although I choose to strive to be as open as possible, not everyone feels or believes the way I do. I need to remember to take their feelings into consideration.

I know there are no secrets. It is important for me to keep my words and actions congruent with my thoughts and beliefs. I believe that a good deal of the peace I have in my life comes from living in truth and alignment. Peaceful people have no secrets!

h
o
n
e
s
t
y

Saying "No"

Saying "no" seems to be a difficult or uncomfortable experience for many people. I don't find it as difficult as some, but I often feel the need to offer an excuse when I say "no" to someone . . . as if it is not okay to say "no" without a good enough reason. Who decides what reason is "good enough?" Society? Why not us?

For example, if we say "no" to something that takes time, there is a hierarchy of acceptable priorities for our time: work, family needs, family obligations, illness, and prior commitments. Isn't it interesting that, for the most part, work comes before family and illness sometimes takes priority ahead of work and family? Where does what *we* need or want fit in to that? (No wonder we get sick when there are a lot of demands on our time.)

When I feel the need to provide a reason or excuse for saying "no," I am often tempted to lie so that I can provide an "acceptable" reason. Why? Do I not want to hurt their feelings? Do I feel that my reason for saying "no" isn't good enough? Do I feel guilty for putting my own needs and wants first? All of the above?

What does this do to my integrity? My self-respect? My relationship with the person I lied to? Is it worth it?

The flip side of the coin is when we place someone in the position of saying "no" by asking for something from them. How many times have we felt uncomfortable asking for something from someone? We place that person in the uncomfortable position of saying "no." If we ask something of someone and they say "yes," do we incur a reciprocal obligation? What if they say "yes" but they really want to say "no?" Do we feel guilty if we know it? What if they say "no" and then lie about why—especially if we find out it was a lie?

No wonder we have trouble asking for what we want in life! There are hidden currents that spin a web of dishonesty in our relationships. The key to clearing away these webs is simple: HONESTY.

With Honesty, there does not need to be any difficulty asking for what we want and saying "no" when we choose. When we have relationships that *value* Honesty, there is freedom. If I ask someone to do something for me and they say "yes," I can be sure they mean it and are doing it because they want to help. If they say "yes," but mean "no," then that is their responsibility, not mine. If I say "yes," and then wish I had said "no," then it is *my* concern, *not* the person who asked.

There is also freedom in saying "no." If I say "no" and am honest about why, I risk hurting someone's feelings. However, when Honesty is valued in the relationship, there is a depth to the relationship that overcomes any momentary disappointment.

honesty

21

For example, a very close friend of mine asked me to come over to her place to celebrate New Year's Eve. I said "no" and stated that I would rather spend New Year's Eve at home. I could have given her a more "acceptable" excuse, but the truth was I wanted to stay home. She may have been disappointed, but our relationship is honest.

What would it be like to live in a world where we were free to ask for what we wanted and free to say "no" when we chose to? Our friends and family would be free to let us know what they needed from us in the way of support, so we wouldn't have to figure out what they needed in silence. We could take risks and ask for outrageous things if we knew people were comfortable saying "no." We could even prioritize our time and energy to include time to take care of ourselves without feeling guilty or getting sick to rest.

All of us do this to some degree. I have many friends on the mainland that are comfortable asking if they can come and stay with me, because they know I will say "no" if it is inconvenient for me. I am free to do the same with them.

In a world where we are honest with each other, there is integrity, abundance, freedom, and a simplicity to our relationships that creates greater depths of trust and love.

two

AVOIDANCE

As I continued on my quest for awareness, I discovered the many ways I avoided things in my life. I would believe that I had made great strides in becoming more aware and conscious of everything going on in my life . . . and then the spiraling journey would bring me back to yet another way I had found to avoid discomfort.

This may not sound like a bad thing to do ... but then I would discover the prices I paid for my avoidance.

Eyes Wide Open

It seems that the more I am honest with myself, the more I am aware of how much I let fear hold me back in my life. An illustration of how often we do hold back is a quote (from the lyrics of a song, I believe): "Dance like no one is watching, and Love like you've never been hurt."

I can dance and look like a fool. There are numerous times when I am not ruled by the fear of looking foolish . . . evidenced by doing things like wearing a clown suit to classes on my last day of college. (The amusing part is that I wasn't trying to make a statement, it was the only clothing still clean in my closet after the end-of-semester crunch!) Yet at other times, I will not voice my opinion about something in case I am wrong. (Heaven forbid that the "brilliant" Maureen is ever wrong!)

When I first learned to do Reiki, I was afraid to express enthusiasm for it, in case it turned out that I was gullible and had spent $150 to simply THINK I could heal with my hands!

One fear that has been dominant in my life is the fear of being hurt emotionally. I think back to many of my relationships, where I held back and didn't open my heart, afraid that my feelings wouldn't be reciprocated, or that he would hurt or disappoint me in some way. How many times have I felt like I could love, only if he loved first?

Another way I hold back is when I feel I have to be in control of my life. I control my life by having a busy schedule, making commitments to others, writing lists, and having my life ruled by my calendar.

A lot of what I find the most satisfying in life is when I lose control. For example, during an orgasm, skydiving, etc.

As I looked at the prices I paid for allowing fear to hold me back, I vividly remembered an experience from my childhood: the Big Dipper Roller Coaster in Vancouver. Each summer I would look at this huge roller coaster, wanting to ride it, but I was too short. Then the summer came when I was tall enough.

I had been looking forward to it for a WHOLE YEAR! All of my cousins were able to ride the year before, since they were tall enough. I FINALLY was tall enough and Dad took me on it. I chattered excitedly in line, then became a little apprehensive as the bar clanked shut in front of me. My hands gripped the bar tightly and then the coaster started to move slowly. I could hear the gears clicking as we started up the steep hill. As we got about a quarter of the way, I started to feel afraid . . . it was really scary and we were high up. I looked ahead to the top of the hill and it seemed like it was miles above us . . . we continued inching up, where the track seemed to end in the sky. The fear built as we approached the very top. My heart was pounding and I looked out and down to the fairground. My stomach seized up in panic . . . I didn't want to be here. I could see the track's path

avoidance

ahead of us . . .straight DOWN! I grabbed the bar across my lap, squeezed my eyes shut, and held my breath as we plummeted to the ground. I kept my eyes closed as we were jerked sideways, shot up and down, and swung around corners—until we started to slow down and came to a stop. As we slowed down, I opened my eyes and saw it was over. My pounding heart relaxed, I took a deep breath, and realized it wasn't all that bad. In fact, it felt rather anticlimactic! I wanted to go again, but Dad absolutely refused. I was frustrated and felt I had been denied the full thrill of the ride. Now that I knew I could do it, I wanted to go back and enjoy it, rather than feeling so afraid that I missed half of the fun.

I sometimes feel like I live my life with my eyes squeezed shut. I hold back and don't commit myself fully to many things. The greatest way I "squeeze my eyes shut" is how I go through life avoiding uncomfortable feelings. I stay busy or distracted whenever I start to feel some anxiety. When something doesn't feel right, I will usually ignore it rather than stay with the feeling. I believe that I miss out on a lot of intuitive awareness when my eyes are "squeezed shut."

Just like I missed the whole visual experience of the roller coaster ride, I know I am missing the Technicolor richness of my life by running away from feelings. When I am not fully engaged in the present moment, with all my senses open and attentive, a lot of what there is to experience in my life passes me by. I would hate to have the same anticlimactic feeling at the end of my life as I did at the end of that first roller coaster ride.

I know I won't always be able to live with my eyes wide open, but the more often I connect to the present moment and open up fully to it, the richer my life will be.

Fear

Fear can be one of the most crippling forces in our lives. When I ask myself what holds me back from so many things, oftentimes the bottom line is fear: Fear of failure, fear of looking foolish (well, I seem to have overcome that one, I often do things that make me look foolish!), fear of feeling uncomfortable (that is a BIG one for me!), fear of being wrong (I prefer to *always* be right!), fear of being judged or rejected, fear of change (which is again a fear of being uncomfortable), fear of the unknown, fear of success (what if I can't keep up with expectations?), and fear of feeling hurt (a major one for me).

As I write this, I see a lack of logic in a lot of my fears. Feeling rejected or hurt is NOT something someone can do to me, rather it is a reaction I CHOOSE to have to someone's words or behavior. All my fears of negative feelings (rejection, hurt, discomfort, etc.) are actually a fear of my OWN CHOICES! Eleanor Roosevelt said, "No one can make you feel inferior without your consent." How true! Only when I *decide* that someone's acceptance or opinion of me is important, is it so.

Other fears are just as illogical. Most of the time they are fears of only a possible (and often unlikely) outcome. There is no guarantee that what we fear will come about. Many times I have heard fear described as:

False Evidence Appearing Real

How many times have we been afraid of something that never occurred? Motivational speaker Bob Proctor quoted Earl Nightingale referring to people ruled by fear: "They tiptoe through life hoping they make it safely to death!" How true! What are we really afraid of? Pain? Failure? Our self-imposed feelings? Dire possibilities we only imagine? Why not imagine the GREAT possibilities?

Many people who know me have described me as brave or courageous. Perhaps in their eyes I am, as they see me do things like bungee jumping, skydiving, speaking in front of groups, and making financial commitments without knowing where the money will come from. There is no courage without great fear. The things that others interpret as courageous are not things that scare me as much as it does them. The times I really feel courageous are the ones where fear comes up, big time: such as risking failure and being open and vulnerable with my feelings with someone.

In August 2000, Reverend Mary Mannin Morrisey spoke in Hawaii and suggested that rather than allowing fear to control our lives, we take it on: not be afraid to make mistakes. She described fear in a positive way: **"Fear is just the border of the reality we've known!"** If I want more satisfaction in my life, if I want things I don't currently have: more intimacy, more money, more laughter, more joy, more friends . . . then the only thing I need to do is take on fear.

How would my life be different if I did not let fear run me so often? Life is all about living without letting fear rule us! Rather than avoid the discomfort of facing fear, what if I embraced it?

Best selling author, Mark Victor Hansen said, "When you take enough action, fear disappears." Could that be because what I fear is not really there? Think back to a moment in your life when you were REALLY AFRAID and you did it anyhow. How about that first kiss, or asking someone out on a date? How about going for the job interview and getting the job? How about walking into a room of people you don't know? We all have had times when we were afraid and stepped through the fear. Once you did, didn't it feel great?

Years ago at a self-improvement seminar, I was shown a diagram that described change. When we face change we have a choice: to perceive change as a threat and avoid it (Going into Fear), or choose to perceive change as an opportunity and get excited (Creating Change).

The first time I went skydiving my heart was racing, I felt shaky, and there was just empty sky in front of me. Then I focused on the desire to be flying through the air. When I jumped out of the plane, I felt an exhilaration that I can still remember many years later. It was great! I want to remember that feeling the next time I feel fear's grasp creeping up on me and embrace a change . . .and DANCE, LIVE, and LOVE, like I've never been hurt!

avoidance

Discipline

Recently the concept of "discipline" has taken on a new twist for me. Previously when I heard the word *discipline*, I thought of something unpleasant, of having to force myself to do something I didn't want to do, but doing it anyway, since I believed it was good for me or I'd like the end result.

In some areas of my life, such as in my work, I have thought of myself as relatively disciplined, in the sense that if I say I will do something, it will get done. In other areas, my self-discipline is inconsistent. For example, I will decide to exercise on a regular basis and do so for a few weeks. At some point, the swimming or walking or whatever activity I had started, disappears from my life. When I dieted, I would be very disciplined, until I reached my target and then I would put the weight back on.

As I looked at this pattern, I realized that in the areas that took what I perceived as discipline, I was forcing myself to do something I didn't want to do. When I was dieting, I would want to eat something that was not on my diet. I would reach for it and stop myself. I would struggle and tell myself "no," that I would not like the consequences on the scale if I ate it. With exercise, I would dread being cold when I got in the pool, or the tired feeling, backache and sore muscles after my walk or workout. I would struggle and tell myself that I would feel worse about myself for not exercising.

I came to see that with this pattern, I was expending a LOT of energy resisting myself. I felt like I was running a marathon, pushing myself a little further, then a little further, always with the finish line in mind. I was willing to expend that amount of energy for a *finite* amount of time, but I couldn't do it *indefinitely*. I couldn't run a marathon every day for the rest of my life.

One day as I was walking, I noticed that as I felt the discomfort of being out of breath and my legs and back hurting, I could take my attention off of my body and distract myself with thoughts about a presentation I was doing. An alarm went off inside!

Over the past few months, one of the things I have been working on is to stay present and connected to my feelings. I have many ways that I use to distract myself from uncomfortable feelings, all of which are quite effective in allowing me to disconnect from what I am feeling at the moment. Here I was doing it while I was walking! I suddenly understood that the mechanism I used to discipline myself was the same one that I had been trying to eliminate in my life. Now what? Was I to give up the idea of having any discipline at all? (I have to admit, that was a tempting thought.)

While writing in my journal, I remembered the experience I had during my bungee jump. As I stood on the platform 140 feet above the river below me, I felt a very visceral fear. I took a few deep breaths and imagined diving off of the little platform. I

avoidance

31

immediately grabbed the railing and knew I wasn't ready to jump. Then my attention shifted to memories of all the times I had been up high somewhere and dreamt of flying freely through the air. As I focused on the desire to feel the exhilaration of flying, my fear disappeared.

I thought about diving off of the platform and the fear welled up again, so I focused on flying; and the desire and exhilaration flowed through me again. When I finally dove off of the platform, I was completely connected to my desire to fly and felt no fear. Not only was it exhilarating, it was thrilling, empowering—and I felt high for two days afterward!

The significant part of this memory, was that I did not RESIST or fight my feeling of fear. Instead, I chose to focus on my DESIRE to fly! This took no discipline on my part, and instead of distracting myself from my fear or ignoring my discomfort, as I tended to think was necessary for discipline, I stayed *very connected* to my feelings and chose to focus on my desire.

My new perspective on discipline is instead of forcing myself to do something uncomfortable and detaching from my discomfort, to stay connected with my feelings of desire for the outcome.

Instead of fighting my desire to eat more than my body needs and feel deprived of the pleasure of food, I can focus on how good it feels to be light and energized without feeling hunger. When I choose to exercise, instead of focusing on the discomfort or dread of the activity, I can focus on being in the fresh air, being present and gentle with my body, and enjoying the sensuality of movement.

For me, discipline is simply a matter of focus—finding my desire in the activity and its outcome and focusing on what I can enjoy in the process. Discipline now becomes an exercise in awareness, rather than a struggle. What a relief!

avoidance

Embracing Change

Lately I seem to be dealing with a lot of change in my life. Usually I resist change, then struggle for a while, and eventually surrender to it. What I hope to get better at is not only surrendering to change, but embracing it. In Beth Terry's book, *Walking in a Crowd of Angels*, she quotes Charles Darwin: "It is not the strongest of the species that survive, nor the most intelligent, but the one most responsive to change." Many people believe that this new millenium is a time of change and transformation in all walks of life.

Some people (myself included) go to great lengths to avoid discomfort, which is almost inevitable when we experience change. Some change is much more uncomfortable than others, such as the death of a loved one, a divorce, or the unexpected loss of a job. The changes I am currently facing are not as dramatic as these events, but I seem to react in a similar way. Sometimes I react to change as a threat, as if it is something to fear rather than an opportunity for something greater. When I am able to shift my perspective and view change as an opportunity, life can get exciting.

I always tell the students in my class that they can't take Reiki without experiencing change in their life on some level. Every time I took a new step in Reiki, I moved and changed jobs. Each time, I knew that the job I had and where I was living was okay, but not ideal. Once I experienced a new level of Reiki, I needed to move. If I didn't choose to move on my own, "circumstances" seemed to push me out the door. I began to realize that when my life was crumbling under my feet, it was because I had refused to step into some change in my life that was (apparently) necessary. I have discovered that if I don't resist it, things move much smoother.

This reminds me of a part in *Illusions*, by Richard Bach, a story about creatures that lived along the bottom of a great crystal river: "Each creature in its own manner clung tightly to the twigs and rocks of the river bottom, for clinging was their way of life, and resisting the current what each had learned from birth . . . one creature said 'I am tired of clinging. Though I cannot see it with my eyes, I trust that the current knows where it is going. I shall let go and let it take me where it will.'" At first the creature was dashed against the rocks and bruised; but in time, it was carried free and flew in the current.

Right now I feel like I am being dragged along by the current and I am not sure where I will end up. Things seem to be moving so swiftly that I can't even focus on what's in front of me. I am in the process of changes in relationships, I am buying a house and moving, I am flying to Europe for a conference, I am organizing my radio show, and still maintaining my regular class and lecture schedule! It dawned on me a few weeks ago, that these changes are a result of a new level of Reiki for myself: I have initiated my first Reiki Master!

When I embrace change, I like to have some time to get used to it. Obviously, that luxury is eluding me right now. I guess I will have to just stay afloat and enjoy the ride. When it slows down enough so my life is not a blur, I will let you know what the scenery is like.

Becoming Authentic

While I was away on a two-month sabbatical, one of my goals was to practice being more aware of my feelings. I believed that there were a lot of subtle feelings and intuitive awareness that I missed because I was frequently distracted by numerous things. Well, I soon discovered that these feelings were not so subtle!

My quest to connect to these feelings began with my therapist when I acknowledged that I often used food to distract me from feeling any uncomfortable emotions. I had (have?) a lot of resistance to allowing those feelings to rise to the surface. I started by becoming aware of the circumstances when I wanted to eat something even though I wasn't physically hungry. (And let me tell you, it still felt like hunger!) I would check in and try to identify what I was feeling. Often, I was feeling agitated or restless, so I would look for something to "fix" the "bad" feelings. I would pace, obsess over incomplete projects, have a glass of wine, and frequently give in and eat. Occasionally I would be more successful and just sit with what I was feeling and write in my journal.

I realized that I was strongly programmed to want to "fix" or avoid feeling anything uncomfortable. I didn't know what to do with these feelings. Of course, the answer is not to DO anything, but to simply feel. I didn't seem to know how to do that.

I also realized that I distracted myself from feeling by being extra busy and having to deal with various crises. My sabbatical gave me a way of minimizing these distractions. It took me a few weeks to settle in, then I began to notice all of my distraction behaviors: checking my e-mail, reading, TV, and food. I wrote in my journal and attempted to find some clarity with my feelings.

What I discovered, to my horror, was that I was becoming quite bitchy! I noticed how many things I went along with simply because someone else wanted me to. I found I had to leave the room when my friend's two-year-old was having a tantrum because I was afraid I would have one, too! In fact, I found that I wanted to retreat to my room more and more. Retreat was a much more comfortable option than confrontation.

I admitted to myself how afraid I was to either disappoint someone or to trigger an angry response. It felt much safer to deny my own desires and accommodate someone else. I became more and more aware of how much I had disregarded my own needs and wants, to the point where I did not even know what I really wanted.

Underlying all of this was a cauldron of seething anger and resentment. I resented the whole world. It was as if all of the years of not respecting my own needs, of negating my own value, and not honoring myself were erupting in a volcanic flow. I wanted to blame someone else, and then I wouldn't have to deal with trying to forgive myself. This was really the key for me, as a lot of this anger was directed towards myself, since I was the one who had betrayed who I truly am.

By this time I was really miserable. I felt stuck between anger and resentment for not getting or doing what I wanted or standing up for myself and being faced with someone's anger or disappointment (and judging myself as selfish at the same time). This really felt like a damned if I do and damned if I don't situation. No matter what I chose, it would be unpleasant and uncomfortable.

At this point I was ready to give in. And some days, I did. It was due to the fact that compromise is sometimes necessary in relationships, and I needed to learn to compromise *and* still voice my desires. Thankfully, the friend I was staying with is a true friend; one who put up with me as I learned to allow my emotions to be present and not be unbearable to be around.

Experiencing my emotions is something like learning how to ice skate . . . it looks easy, but as soon as I take a step forward, there is no control, everything moves too fast, and kaboom! I have a painful fall. While I am sitting on my butt, with the cold ice melting through my clothes, I watch the other skaters. It not only looks easy for them, but they also seem to be enjoying themselves. I decide I have had enough for today. Maybe tomorrow I will try again. I keep telling myself that I will eventually enjoy and appreciate being connected to my emotions.

After recognizing my "angry" feelings, I found that there were times when I had no reluctance to express my anger. I discovered that in some situations, such as in business dealings, I did not hold back. As I examined these feelings more closely, I saw that in those situations I was not afraid of confrontation because

avoidance

I wasn't concerned about whether the person I spoke to liked me or not. So, when I held back, I wasn't really afraid of confrontation or someone's anger, I was afraid of being rejected!

As I watched my friend discipline her daughter one day, she made sure that she communicated that she loved her daughter, that it was her daughter's BEHAVIOR that she was upset with. In other words, separating her response to the behavior from her feelings toward her daughter. My friend pointed out to me that when I am afraid of being rejected for expressing my anger, I am afraid of being rejected for my behavior, not for who I am. I acknowledged that I have this fear because I judge my own worthiness by my behavior and accomplishments, rather than by who I am (more to work on!).

The word I would use to describe someone who is honest with themselves and others about their feelings is "authentic." I realized how I have often been inauthentic when I was easygoing and accommodating. That wasn't being fully honest, although I thought I was. I thought about the people I admire whom I would describe as authentic. They are not always nice and they are not always liked, but they have a depth and a vitality that draws me to them. I find their authenticity refreshing. Part of what I have been feeling lately is a sense of loss, of grief, for the most authentic part of me that has been buried for so long.

Now that I have exhumed my wants and desires and can more easily recognize them, I want to honor them (and therefore, honor myself). In addition, I believe that as I learn to listen to the feelings that rise up for me, I will connect to an inner wisdom. I will feel more clarity and confidence in the choices I make, as I allow myself to feel the "resonance" of my choices . . . to know what is right for me. I know that when something doesn't feel right, I can discover what is out of alignment with my own needs and wants, and then I can communicate what feels right for me.

I have wondered how much energy I have used in suppressing all of these uncomfortable feelings. I expect that as I allow my feelings to flow naturally, I may find a wellspring of additional energy.

It still takes courage to face my fear of people's anger and rejection. I may disappoint some people when I am not as "nice" as I used to be. But I know I will emerge as my authentic self: the woman who is vital, dynamic, and knows what she wants.

avoidance

three

ATTITUDE

During my introspective times it has become obvious to me that my attitude colors everything I experience.

There are times when I am in a funk and I can't seem to pull myself out of it, or more honestly, I don't want to pull myself out of it. Perhaps I want to wallow in self-pity, savor a little anger, or simply I am too fatigued to shift my perspective.

Often attitude boils down to whether we see the glass half empty or half full. I discovered that whatever perspective I took, it became a habit. I noticed there were times when I expected the worst from someone and spent my energy bracing myself for it. Other times, after a little practice, I could see the positive aspect in almost every situation. After I practiced looking for the good in each situation, it started to become a habit.

Having a positive outlook on things was a good beginning yet, as I looked more closely, I found evidence of some pessimism creeping up in my behavior. Eventually, I discovered that not only did I need to look for the bright side, and expect the best rather than the worst, but I also had to find within me the ability to TRUST in the positive.

Choice is Everything

The following article, sent to me by my friend Joy, says it all:

Jerry was the kind of guy you love to hate. He was always in a good mood and always had something positive to say. When someone would ask him how he was doing, he would reply, "If I were any better, I would be twins!"

He was a unique manager because he had several waiters who followed him around from restaurant to restaurant. The reason the waiters followed Jerry was because of his attitude. He was a natural motivator. If an employee was having a bad day, Jerry was there, telling the employee how to look on the positive side of the situation.

Seeing this style really made me curious, so one day I went up to Jerry and asked him, "I don't get it! You can't be a positive person all of the time. How do you do it?"

Jerry replied, "Each morning I wake up and say to myself, 'Jerry, you have *two choices* today. You can choose to be in a good mood or you can choose to be in a bad mood.' I choose to be in a good mood. Each time something bad happens, *I can choose to be a victim or I can choose to learn from it.* I choose to learn from it. Every time someone comes to me complaining, I can choose to accept their complaining or I can point out the positive side of life. I choose the positive side of life."

"Yeah, right, but it's not that easy," I protested.

"Yes it is," Jerry said. **"Life is all about choices. When you cut away all the junk, every situation is a choice.** You choose how you react to situations. You choose how people will affect your mood. You choose to be in a good or a bad mood. The bottom line: It's your choice how you live life."

I reflected on what Jerry said. Soon thereafter, I left the restaurant industry to start my own business. We lost touch, but I often thought about him when I made a choice about life instead of reacting to it.

Several years later, I heard that Jerry did something you are never supposed to do in a restaurant business: he left the back door open one morning and was held up at gunpoint by three armed robbers. While trying to open the safe, shaking from nervousness, his hand slipped off the lock. The robbers panicked and shot him.

Luckily, Jerry was found relatively quickly and rushed to the local trauma center. After 18 hours of surgery and weeks of intensive care, Jerry was released from the hospital with fragments of the bullets still in his body. I saw Jerry about six months after the accident. When I asked him how he was, he replied, "If I were any better, I'd be twins. Wanna see my scars?" I declined to see his wounds, but did ask him what had gone through his mind as the robbery took place. "The first thing that went through my mind was that I should have locked the back door," Jerry replied. "Then, as I lay on the floor, I remembered that I had two choices: I could choose to live or I could choose to die. I chose to live."

"Weren't you scared? Did you lose consciousness?" I asked.

He continued, "The paramedics were great. They kept

a
t
t
i
t
u
d
e

telling me I was going to be fine. But when they wheeled me into the emergency room and I saw the expressions on the faces of the doctors and nurses, I got really scared. In their eyes, I read, 'He's a dead man.' I knew I needed to take action."

"What did you do?" I asked.

"Well, there was a big, burly nurse shouting questions at me," said Jerry. "She asked if I was allergic to anything. 'Yes,' I replied. The doctors and nurses stopped working as they waited for my reply. I took a deep breath and yelled, 'Bullets!' Over their laughter, I told them, 'I am choosing to live. Operate on me as if I am alive, not dead.'"

Jerry lived, thanks to the skill of his doctors, but also because of his amazing attitude. *I learned from him that every day we have the choice to live fully.*

Choosing our Attitude is everything.

Perception Creates Our Reality

I recently noticed that my outlook on life and how I perceived my reality could be shifted by something as simple as an e-mail message. I received an e-mail telling me that a check I was expecting was on its way. That one simple message altered my whole outlook for the week! In truth, nothing had changed in my life, I just expected things to be easier the following week, and so they were! Why can't I have that same expectation without being so dependent on external events?

There are so many unplanned things that can happen to make my life more enjoyable, why shouldn't I live with the expectation that they will? And, if a magical surprise doesn't materialize, I still had a joyful week and the magical surprise is probably just around the corner! In fact, if I keep expecting a magical surprise to appear I am sure it will. As I've said before, "To think is to create."

I remember many years ago when I had put on some weight and was up to 170 pounds. I felt very fat, unattractive, and was ashamed of my body. I hated how my clothes fit and knew that no man would be interested in me. Guess what? It was true! I became quite depressed and things didn't get any better in the rest of my life either. Over the following year I gradually gained another 30 pounds and weighed over 200 pounds.

At that point I decided to participate in a 90-day weight loss program. I dropped 30 pounds in 90 days! I felt great! I felt lighter, freer, more attractive, and sure enough, I began dating again.

The most interesting aspect of all of this was that I felt (and was) attractive at 170 pounds . . . the same weight that over a year before had depressed me. THE ONLY DIFFERENCE WAS MY PERSPECTIVE. In fact, I remember many years ago weighing 140 pounds and being ashamed of my body!

This reminds me that my PERCEPTION of a situation is what makes it real. The only reality is right now, this moment. How I view my past and how I anticipate my future both color my experience in this moment. The exciting part is that I CHOOSE MY PERSPECTIVE, therefore I can create my reality exactly as I choose. How empowering!

The first step for me is to "check in" and see what my current perspective is. How joyful and grateful am I? How empowered do I feel? How do I anticipate my day and week will be? Am I avoiding anything? Do I feel stuck in any way? Once I check in, I can see if I want to change my reality and adjust my perspective.

There are times when I know I need to shift and I find it difficult to do. Some of the things that help me are:

    ◎ Watch an inspiring movie. A good movie will take my awareness completely out of my own life and put my petty concerns back where they belong. (*Gandhi* is a great movie for me.)

⚙ Read inspiring books, such as *Chicken Soup for the Soul.*

⚙ Help others. If I am feeling sorry for myself or down, all I need to do is be of service to others and I immediately feel better. As a hospice volunteer, helping people who are facing death or the loss of a loved one, I am rewarded with a clear picture of the priorities in my life. When serving meals to the homeless, I can't help but be grateful for all of the abundance in my life.

⚙ Listen to music. I will play upbeat music if I am feeling lethargic. I am best motivated to do housework by rock and roll or reggae music.

⚙ Spend some time in nature. Going for a solitary walk on the beach or in the mountains always gives me a fresh perspective.

⚙ Watch children play (or play with them). Life is so new and exciting through a child's eyes.

attitude

The point of all of this is that we really do create our reality and we can consciously choose to create whatever we want. We are NEVER victims of our circumstances and the only thing separating us from a joyful and happy life is how we choose to see ourselves and our current circumstances.

I am so grateful that my life becomes easier and more fulfilling every day. I know yours will too, because that is what my perception is!

Gratitude

On New Year's Day, 1998, I spent some time reviewing my experiences the previous year and was almost overwhelmed by how much I had to be grateful for. Even the death of my father a few weeks earlier brought me much more peace than pain.

I am blessed with a life that gets better and better each year. In 1997 I met hundreds of new people, and have found some new, lifelong friends. I have experienced deeper intimacy, honesty, and trust in many of my relationships. My work is something I love and continues to grow. Most of all, I am recognizing the countless miracles that occur in my daily life.

Many of these miracles have been happening all along, but I just didn't notice. Sometimes the miracle is simple, like making it to an appointment on time when I didn't leave early enough. Other times it is more dramatic, such as avoiding an accident by noticing something a split second early enough. My favorite ones, though, are the simple things that make my life flow easily, like remembering an important folder I left on my desk when I am two steps out the front door, instead of an hour away.

The magic of these miracles is that when I notice and acknowledge them, they multiply! As I often say in class, "Energy flows where our attention goes." When I pay attention to these "little" miracles, they grow! I believe that by culturing gratitude in my life, I feed all of these miracles. I can choose to focus on the obstacles or voids in my life, or I can choose to focus on what is working and what I have. When I focus on what is working, I am able to see that the universe is infinitely abundant—with love, with solutions, and with miracles! When I recognize this, I attract more abundance. The abundance is always there, but when I deny its existence I block its ability to flow in my life.

I started my usual New Year's resolutions list, which included things like exercising at least three times a week, and then I stopped. I don't need to make promises to myself that, based on past results, I may not fulfill. If I want different results, I need to approach things differently. So instead of resolutions, what I decided to do for myself is keep a daily gratitude journal. I take a few minutes each day to acknowledge a few things I am grateful for. I believe that this one, simple, daily ritual can be more powerful and transformational than having the discipline to keep a dozen other resolutions.

As the power of gratitude is nurtured in my life, all things (including regular exercise!) become easier.

Living Our Passion

I am grateful each day that I have discovered my path and passion in life: teaching Reiki. Life is not only more rewarding than I thought it would be, but easier, too. I believe that life is not meant to be a struggle, but to be a joyful unfolding.

My life was much more of a struggle when I was working in a career that I was capable of doing, but not using my unique gifts fully. It took a lot of energy and effort to discipline myself to do the things my job required. There is still a place for discipline in my life, but I am not paddling my canoe *against* the current and struggling anymore. I feel like I am riding a canoe *with* the current. I simply guide my choices and correct my course from time to time. Often I feel like I have put forth no effort and I am carried forward in a wave of delight!

Finding our path needn't be difficult. In fact, for me, it was a process of discovery. I didn't figure it out and then choose it. Instead, I eventually discovered that I was already there!

I did not suddenly say "aha!" when I took First Degree Reiki.

In fact, when I first learned Reiki, I was fairly skeptical and wasn't sure anything was happening when I did Reiki for someone. I later decided to take Second Degree—because my Reiki Master was in town, not because I was aware of any particular calling in life.

In retrospect, what was most interesting is that I decided to take Second Degree when I *didn't* feel a strong desire to learn more about Reiki. It was as if I made the decision unconsciously. A few years later I made the decision to train as a Reiki Master.

The reason I made such a significant commitment was because of an experience I had while auditing a class—I felt overwhelming love for everyone in the class and I experienced everyone in their perfection. I knew that being in that loving place was where I was meant to be. I simply wanted more of that experience and so the only other step available with Reiki was to train as a Master.

The experience I had was an awakening to my passion. My desire for more of that experience led me to where I am today. At the time I made the decision to become a Reiki Master, I still expected to continue in the same career path. I viewed my work with Reiki as simply a step in my spiritual growth, not a career decision. It was not until the latter part of my year of preparation that I realized that teaching Reiki was all I wanted to do.

When I am teaching Reiki I usually experience that same overwhelming love for each person. It is similar to when we look into an infant's eyes and see their innocence and perfection. This experience is so nourishing to my soul, that everything else becomes easy.

attitude

The point of all of this is that when we follow our hearts, or our spirit, we will be led in the direction of fulfillment.
Sometimes, the fact that we don't know where we are being led adds to the joy of it all. It is like being blindfolded and led into an exciting, new adventure.

Connecting to my path has been an ongoing process of **surrender** and **letting go**:

- of my need to feel in control of my life
- of wanting to know what lies ahead
- of knowing how I will accomplish what I need to
- of expecting things to turn out as I have anticipated

The key to being successful in this surrender is **TRUST**. When I trust the flow of the river of my life, things will work out better than when I follow what my current, limited viewpoint can show me. I have had numerous experiences of letting go and trusting and having things fall into an even better outcome than what I thought I wanted. It is trust in the Divine wisdom.

In addition, when I let go of my need to know and control where my life takes me, each day becomes a delight of new surprises! (And I LOVE surprises!)

My wish is for all of you to experience the joy and fullness of living life in the path of the universal river of life.

LET GO and enjoy the ride!

The Power of Surrender

 When I used to think about surrender, I felt it implied weakness and giving up. How wrong I was! I have learned that surrender can be the most empowering action I can take.

It all depends on what we surrender to.

When I was dieting, I used to surrender to my cravings, to my feelings of deprivation, to my desire for instant gratification, to my frustration. When I was exercising, I used to surrender to my lethargy, my sore muscles, and the discomfort of the moment. When I was in college, I used to surrender to my procrastination, my boredom, and my self-doubt. In other words, whenever I faced a challenging situation, I thought surrender was giving in to whatever I felt I was fighting.

That was where I gave up my power. In martial arts, it is taught that rather than fighting the force of an opponent's energy, the key is to go with it and use their own energy and direct the flow. Then you are in control! When we resist something, we give it control. (What we resist, persists. . and again, Energy flows where our attention goes.)

Rather than surrender to an obstacle or an opponent, I can choose to surrender to my success. For example, at a seminar I attended, I learned a very simple and powerful definition of commitment: "Commitment is making a choice and surrendering to it —100%!" What that means is that once I COMMIT myself to something, whether it be a diet, a marriage, or a career, I only need to make the choice once, then I SURRENDER to it. I never have to be faced with a decision on a diet, such as "should I eat that chocolate cake or should I eat an apple instead?" Or "do I really want to be in this marriage?" I have already decided. It is a no-brainer. I don't have to struggle with willpower or choices. It is so much easier, so freeing, and SO EMPOWERING!

I can choose to surrender to honoring my ability to know my own truth and to my greatness. When I do surrender, life becomes so easy. Whenever life is a struggle, all I have to do is find what I am resisting or fighting and surrender to a positive aspect of myself, and the power of the universe is then free to flow through me and life becomes good.

Sometimes surrendering is a matter of letting go of having things work out the way I *think* they should be. Usually when I let go (i.e., let go and let God), things work out in ways I never even imagined they would! SURRENDER to your highest and enjoy the support of the universe.

Spiritual Optimism

Intellectually, I get a lot of this stuff. In fact, I can spout it off in every newsletter. I can counsel friends and appear very wise and positive. Yet, to truly LIVE it, to "walk my talk," and to EMBODY this "Spiritual Optimism" has been much more challenging.

I had lots of practice redirecting my thinking to more positive perspectives. I considered myself an optimist, and most others did, too. When I was forced to take a closer look, I realized that my thinking, my feelings and my actions were not congruent. In fact, they were often contradictory!

Einstein was once asked what he thought was the most important question a person needed to answer. His response was: "Is the universe a friendly place or not?" I believed that I viewed the universe as a friendly place . . . yet, I was afraid to experience my feelings. I was afraid to be vulnerable and risk getting hurt in my relationships and I was afraid to commit to something if I wasn't totally sure I would be successful at it. I had little patience, which I passed off as a desire for instant gratification. Did this not reflect a lack of trust that all I desired would eventually come to be?

It was a rude awakening to realize how divergent my thoughts and actions (therefore my beliefs) were! I had to admit that I *did not* behave or function from a BELIEF that the universe was a friendly or safe place . . . but I THOUGHT it was so!

This contradiction can be viewed from a "vibrational" perspective. We can first change our frequency on the level of thought. Thoughts move quickly and have a light frequency, but as we move into our emotions, the vibration becomes a little thicker and denser, sort of sticky. It is more difficult to move and change. Finally, we come to the physical vibration, which is very dense (some of us more so than others, perhaps) and more resistant to change.

So, how do we come into alignment? For some, it can happen quickly, like an epiphany. They suddenly GET that which they think is indeed true and their world shifts for them. Sometimes it is described as a spiritual awakening, experiencing God's presence and feeling completely safe. (I have longed for that experience.) When mythologist Joseph Campbell was asked if he was a man of faith, he laughed and said he didn't need faith because he had experience!

For others, who resist change on each level, like myself (it is amazing I have any fingernails left, as I typically hold on tightly to where I am at, until the pain of my torn fingernails is unbearable), it can take a "dark night of the soul" as described by Joan Borysenko in her book, *Fire in the Soul*, when staying where we are becomes so painful that we let go and begin to embrace life in a different way.

Not long ago I emerged from a "dark night" and am beginning to see the dawn. I anticipate the outcome will be that I am
living more in alignment with my thoughts, emotions, and my
body . . . and I will have discovered the "Friendly" universe I live in.

a
t
t
i
t
u
d
e

four

GIVING

There are times when I find it easier to give than at other times. When I am optimistic and feel good about myself, giving is easy. When I have an abundance of time, money, and resources, giving is easy. What I have discovered, though, is that giving is good for me . . . things seem to flow full circle. As I give, I reinforce my belief in abundance. The ultimate giving is forgiving . . . "giving as before," especially ourselves.

Energy and Giving

In Reiki classes we talk about how important the exchange of energy is when doing Reiki. Many of us are more comfortable giving of ourselves than receiving from others. This is partly due to cultural influences. When we receive from others we may feel obligated in some way, or we may feel we are being selfish.

Have you ever stopped to think about the times you were able to do something for someone else? Have you noticed the warm feeling in your heart when someone sincerely thanks you for something you've done? Do you remember the joy and satisfaction of seeing the excitement of someone when you have given them a gift?

All of these experiences would not be possible if the recipient of your giving was not open to receiving. Often the greatest gift you can give someone is to joyfully receive what they have given to you.

Many times we give with no desire or opportunity to receive something in return. Although we know that what we give will come back to us, sometimes we feel depleted or that the giving is not balanced in some way. This imbalance can be created if someone does not receive joyfully or gratefully. It can also be created if we are not equally open to receiving.

If you have experienced a sense of imbalance, ask yourself: How open have you been to receiving? How often have you asked for what you want from others? Do you joyfully let people give to you?

Our physical heart is a perfect example of the flow of energy. It constantly pumps, giving and receiving, giving and receiving. If the blood does not flow, the heart stops and we die. It is the same with energy. It needs to constantly flow between each other, giving and receiving, giving and receiving. If the giving or the receiving is blocked, a "heart attack" occurs—we experience pain in our "emotional hearts."

The flow of energy amongst each other is as important to life as the flow of blood to the heart. It is the beating of the universal heart: giving and receiving, giving and receiving, giving and receiving, giving and receiving, giving and receiving, giving and receiving . . . giving and receiving . . . giving and receiving, giving and receiving, giving and receiving . . .

g
i
v
i
n
g

Forgiveness

One day I reflected on how blessed I was to have so many people in my life that loved me unconditionally. I savored the warm, rich feeling of their love.

I then thought about other people in my life that I knew loved me unconditionally, and I realized that I didn't get the same feeling from them. Why was that? In the past I would have assumed that they didn't truly love me unconditionally, or that there was something lacking in what they were giving me that affected how much love they could give.

I realized that it wasn't something in *them* that affected the love I was receiving, but rather it was something within *me*! Even though they loved me as unconditionally as the others, I couldn't feel it in the same warm way—because I wouldn't let it in! Why? I realized there was an aspect of myself that was afraid of opening up completely to these people.

To receive unconditional love fully from someone, we need to open our hearts up fully to them. I was afraid I would be hurt! Why then was I able to open my heart to some but not to all? Obviously, I didn't trust some. Again, why?

As I thought about my fear of opening up and sensed my lack of trust, I began to recall times when that person had hurt me in the past. A lot of these hurts were from long ago and not really significant. I discovered that even though I *thought* I had let go of these hurts, I was still holding onto them . . . I HAD NOT COMPLETELY FORGIVEN THESE PEOPLE!

I finally understood that as long as I remained unforgiving, I was blocked to receiving the unconditional love these people had for me, as I couldn't open my heart to let it in!

So, whenever I want to experience love more deeply in my life, I know I simply need to look to where I need to forgive more.

How do we forgive more? I thought I had forgiven these people. It was only when I looked closely that I discovered I was still holding hurt and resentment. I think one of the reasons these things were hidden from my awareness is that I have a tendency to avoid uncomfortable emotions. As noted in the previous section on avoidance, I can be quite adept at avoiding discomfort!

So the first step in forgiveness is being aware that we have something to forgive. How do you do this?

I don't know that I have the answer to this question, although I know some things that work for me: the first is to look at the person I need to forgive and consider their perspective in the situation. Why would they behave in a way that would hurt me? For the most part, I find that they did not have malicious intent. Their behavior was either a reflex or thoughtlessness. It is much easier for me to forgive when I know the intent was not to hurt me.

My mother once suggested that people behave in hurtful ways because that same behavior is what they experienced, just as someone who is abusive was almost always abused themselves.

The second thing that works for me, especially if there is a possibility that the person really did want to hurt me, is to look for their fear. I believe the only time someone can wish harm to another is when they are hurting and fearful themselves. Anytime I look at someone doing something hurtful; I find the fear that is driving their behavior. When I see that they are in more pain than I am, it is easier to feel compassion and forgiveness.

The final step is to remember that I am the one who chooses to feel hurt. The truth is, no one can hurt me, as I am responsible for how I choose to respond to their behavior. I remember as a child bursting into tears when my mother spoke sharply. My sister, on the other hand, would look at her as if to say, "There she goes again!" and didn't react! I was amazed at how my sister saw it as my mother's problem and not hers.

If you think of a young child that is frustrated and angry, who says that he hates you and strikes out, it is easy to feel compassion for the child's struggle, and not feel hurt by their behavior. The adults in our lives are no different.

The more whole and complete I am within myself, the more I am able to feel open and trusting toward others. If I am the one who decides whether to feel hurt or not, then I don't have to be fearful of others. The result is I can experience more love in my life, all because I am able to let go and recognize that my hurts come from within.

The REAL Bottom Line

The following are examples from business people who demonstrated a refreshing perspective on work and career:

⑥ One woman turned down one of her largest contracts ever, because she felt her client would not treat her respectfully.

⑥ Another woman stood her ground with a client and would not compromise her professional integrity to keep her client happy.

⑥ A business owner discovered that an employee was stealing from her. Rather than looking only at the security of her operations, she also looked at where her business was out of balance and attracting theft.

⑥ Many others have left high-paying, successful positions to do something that brings them more joy.

I believe in supporting other Reiki Masters in their work and encouraging people I meet to study with the Master they connect with best. Instead of seeing other Reiki Masters as competition, I see them as colleagues. I see us sharing the vision of health and peace that Reiki can bring to others. Rather than having a perspective of lack: the view that if an individual learns Reiki from someone else, it means one less student for me, I see things from abundance. When someone connects with the right Reiki Master for them, they will tell many others about their good experiences, indirectly creating more potential students for us all. It is this Real Bottom Line that I see unfolding in our society that is truly exciting.

None of these things are new. People have made decisions like these before, but the exciting news is that there is a definite shift to new priorities in business, which reflect a more holistic perspective: *The REAL Bottom Line.*

More businesses are donating money and services to their communities, and instead of being concerned about how much goodwill or exposure the donation will "buy," they simply donate because they are aware of the *energy* that these contributions produce.

In the past, when business people made decisions, they would primarily take into consideration the profitability of a situation. That is still important, but today we often see other factors come into play during the decision-making process. Integrity, self-respect, and personal satisfaction are often ahead of income when people consider career choices; and they are also being valued equally with profit by businesses.

There is an awareness of the flow of energy that everything we do produces. As businesses work for Win-Win situations for everyone, we all tap into the abundant, infinite flow of the universe.

Once the business world acknowledges that there are many unseen factors that affect success, we will all function from a more REAListic Bottom Line. I congratulate and cheer all of you who are living your work from a fuller, more holistic perspective.

Daily I am grateful for the opportunity to do work that I passionately love, that I get to travel and visit dear friends on the mainland, meet new people every week, and affect other people's lives with my work. It is my dream that everyone will be in such a position soon.

g
i
v
i
n
g

Being of Service

Knowing that I have been of service and really helped someone always gives me deep, lasting pleasure. (In contrast to chocolate, the pleasure of which dissipates within minutes!)

There are times when I am asked to 'be of service' and I want to pull back or withdraw. Why? There are two very different situations when I feel this way. The first is when I feel that the person who is asking for my assistance will keep drawing from me until I am depleted. It is as if this person is so needy that if I give a little, they will never stop, and I feel a need to protect myself. There is something unbalanced about the flow of energy between us.

When I take a step back and look at why I feel this way, I realize that this person, in some way, has disempowered himself or herself and is feeling a deep lack from within. It is as if they don't believe they have enough to give to others. In this type of situation, I feel I can be of more service when I assist them in seeing how capable they are, rather than doing something for them.

The other times when I pull back is when I am out of balance myself and my own life force energy is at a low level. This is when I feel overwhelmed if anyone asks anything of me. In this situation I need to take some time for myself, do some Reiki, and even ask for support from others. (Asking for something from others is still difficult for me.)

Being in this state can be more detrimental than we realize. Unfortunately, it is a common situation, and a reflection of the fact that we are energetically diminished. When we are whole and well, we have exuberance for life and a natural desire to give of ourselves. Each day we do not feel this way, we lose the precious opportunity to live our lives richly, fully, and joyfully.

What makes life joyful, rich, and fulfilling is knowing we have contributed to others in some way. I expect when I die, people are not going to look back on my life and remember how clean my house was, how much money I made, or even how accomplished I was. What I expect people will remember is how many lives I touched, how many I served. (Of course, I also expect to have earned a reputation for being a little outrageous and eccentric in my later years!)

I have learned that whenever I am in a funk, depressed, or simply have lost perspective, getting out and helping others in even the simplest ways works miracles.

I recently overheard someone say to another person, "Thank you for letting me be of service." I was reminded that it is a gift to accept (and ask for!) assistance from others. I am so grateful to all the people who allow me into their lives and let me know how I can be of service to them. I am the one who receives the most when I see that my efforts make a difference. The best thank you I can get is when someone accepts what I have to offer joyfully, without feeling any burden or awkwardness. This is very

giving

different from the one I mentioned above, where a person feels disempowered. There is no awkwardness when the recipient of my efforts knows that they will be able to return the favor in some way, if not to me, then to someone else.

In *The Seven Spiritual Laws of Success,* Deepak Chopra says: "Everyone has a purpose in life . . . a unique gift or special talent to give to others. And when we blend this unique talent with service to others, we experience the ecstasy and exultation of our own spirit, which is the ultimate goal of all goals."

When we view life from a perspective of "What can I give?" we are coming from a place of abundance. If we view things from "What's in it for me?" we are in a place of limits and deficiencies. It is harder to perceive abundance when we are experiencing a lack of energy in our lives. This is one opportunity for Reiki to bring more abundance and prosperity into our lives. When we nourish and replenish ourselves with Reiki, it is much easier to say: "What can I give?" The more open we are to giving and being of service, the more we allow the flow of universal abundance into our lives.

The next step is to be ready for this abundance and to joyfully and gratefully receive all that is offered to us. In this way, the energy keeps flowing and all of us prosper and benefit.

Being Unconditional

When we are unconditional, we are set free. What I mean is that when we are truly being unconditional, our happiness is not dependent on anything else.

For example, when we give something to someone unconditionally, we give it ALL to them. Have you given someone a gift with the hope that they *really* like it? That is not unconditional, as our pleasure in giving is dependent on how the other person receives it! Do you expect the person to thank you and express some appreciation or gratitude? If I give a gift and the recipient later gives it to someone else, I can usually feel okay about it. But what if they give it to a thrift store? What if they throw it out? If I do not completely let go of all my expectations about the gift, I am not being unconditional.

Much is written and said about unconditional love, but we do not often give or receive it. When we are in a relationship with someone and we feel love for them, we want them to love us in return.

A mother's love for her child is often said to be unconditional, since the child is loved just because he is her child. Yet, many times the mother has expectations about her child's life, choices, behavior, etc. Often a parent feels responsible for their child's success, or that the child is a reflection of how good a parent they are. When a parent feels pride for their child, it is a reflection of expectations, not unconditional love.

I have a few friends that I feel unconditional love for. If you asked me *why* I love them, I could not answer, because I just feel the love. They don't have to phone me, remember my birthday, or do anything at all. I just feel overwhelming love for them. One of the reasons I feel this love is that I feel I know who they really are, that I see ALL of them. Perhaps it is a reflection of myself that I see in them.

I know I want to be loved unconditionally, but I still find that I expect myself to be perfect in order to be worthy of love! How absurd! I don't expect those that I love to be 'perfect' in fact, some of the most loveable aspects of the people in my life are their imperfections! Yet whenever I am feeling down on myself, guilty, or disappointed that someone didn't respond to me the way I'd hoped (maybe I didn't get the contract I had proposed, or the new man I met chose to be with someone else), underneath all of the bad feelings about myself is the feeling that if I don't do or be all of the right things, then I don't deserve to be loved!

The most valuable part of being unconditional is to love ourselves unconditionally! When we can do that, it is easy to be unconditional with others. We don't feel we need anything, as we are complete. This, I believe, is what is said to be God's unconditional love.

five
SELF-JUDGEMENT

The major obstacle to loving myself unconditionally is self-judgement. This monster creeps up on me all the time. I catch myself berating myself for things, expecting myself to be perfect, and not believing that I am worthy of what I desire; unless I change all the things I have criticized myself for.

I still struggle with the idea that I can be loved simply because I AM, rather than because of behaviors or attributes that make me lovable.

What a concept!

Self-Judgement

I recently became aware that I live my life by a double standard: I have a certain set of standards that I expect myself to live up to and another, more forgiving, perspective that I view others with.

I think most of us agree that we are usually our own worst critics, but I didn't realize how pervasive and judgmental this criticism is. It includes all the times I impose "shoulds" or "shouldn'ts" on myself: "I *should* be doing something productive rather than reading this magazine." "I *should* be eating fruit and vegetables instead of this ice cream." "I *should* have done my laundry yesterday when I said I would." "I *shouldn't* be going to a movie, I *should* be unpacking my boxes!"

I also noticed that whenever I felt like keeping something secret (or private) about myself, such as the chocolate I ate in bed, the amount of time I "wasted" playing solitaire on the computer, and the fast-food wrappers in the car, I would hide the evidence. I was afraid of what others would think about me because I had *already* harshly judged myself! In fact, I discovered that everything I didn't want someone else to know about me was based upon a fear of being judged by them . . . as I had done to myself.

Then I thought, "Well, if I am ashamed of this behavior or afraid of others' judgments of me, perhaps I should change my behavior . . . clean up my act, so to speak." This kind of thinking is what has perpetuated my self-judgement: expecting myself to live up to a standard of perfection that is impossible!

This is where I began to notice my double standard. I expect myself to be *perfect* in order to be *worthy* of respect, love, recognition, joy, and pleasure; yet I do not have that same standard for others. In fact, when I notice the imperfections in other people, I often find it a relief. I find it endearing that they are not perfect . . . it makes them not only forgivable but also more lovable!

My judgments also include the thoughts I have about myself: "I'm too fat." "I am lazy." "I am being selfish." "I am messy." "I am clumsy." etc. At times this escalates into name-calling: "Stupid!" "Ugly!" "Slob!"

I would **NEVER** call someone else hurtful names. I wasn't even aware that I did it to myself, until I REALLY started to pay attention. This name-calling was SO automatic and common that I didn't consciously hear it. I was shocked at what kind of conversations were going on in my mind without my noticing.

Now, I like having high standards to live up to, and I admire and respect others who have high standards for themselves and others, but, to live by such a double standard, to be so unforgiving of myself, and to be so harsh and cruel in my thoughts, is not only unhealthy, but harmful!

Perhaps I started being judgmental about myself to antici-

self-judgement

pate and avoid criticism from others. By subjecting myself to the pain first, somehow made it less scary. It also gave me an opportunity to "correct" myself before I was judged by others. This habit grew out of control, like a cancer that has spread and is harming my health.

These harsh, judgmental thoughts eat away at my self-esteem like salt water corrodes iron—even the strongest piece of iron will crumble into dust over time. When I am fearful that others will see my imperfections, I am less genuine and open. When I hold a double standard, I cannot experience deep intimacy, as I am somehow "different" from another. The names I call myself are hurtful. Where does the pain go when I am not even aware that I am hurt? (Into my body, perhaps?) And most of all, when I am judgmental and unforgiving of myself, how much abundance, love, and joy have I missed because I haven't felt worthy and been open to receiving all of the blessings of life?

I need to treat myself the way I would treat my dearest friends—with compassion, honesty, and forgiveness. We can all use more of that in our lives.

Not Enough

I seem to constantly struggle with feeling that what I am doing (and sometimes who I am) is not enough. When I look at the balance in my checkbook, for example, I chastise myself that I am not doing enough to reach the students who want Reiki. I am not sending out regular announcements about my classes, or I haven't got my new business cards printed yet, or my Web site is out of date . . . or maybe, in those deep dark periods of self-doubt, no matter how hard I seem to try, perhaps I **am not enough!!!!**

In my relationships with friends, I often feel pangs of guilt when I forget to acknowledge a birthday or I don't answer an e-mail promptly. Sometimes I am not really there for a friend because I am feeling overwhelmed by the pressure of all my unfinished tasks (which are self-induced, since I haven't *done enough*). When months go by without seeing or talking with a friend I tell myself I haven't done enough to nurture the friend-ship, that I haven't made this person enough of a priority in my life to call and say hello or to meet for lunch.

This seems to be pervasive in all areas of my life. Even when

I am doing things successfully, I tend to harshly judge my attempts and focus on what I could have done more, or better. For example, when I go for a walk, I may walk for 20 minutes. Instead of congratulating myself for walking for the first time in 3 weeks, I focus on "only 20 minutes." As I write this it sounds so extreme, but I must confess that I do this way too often.

I even avoid acknowledging the strides I make in my life, out of an irrational fear that if I acknowledge that I can do this, then I will be expected to do more! (Expected by whom? Myself, of course!)

Why do I do this to myself? Besides a slightly neurotic need to be an over-achiever, there is a part of me that is afraid of being wrong and humbled, of praising myself and then discovering that perhaps I wasn't so great after all. Not to mention that others may reject me for appearing **conceited**. In fact, my second grade report card states in black and white that my behavior was unacceptable as I was too conceited! Can you imagine, a seven-year-old child being **too conceited**?! I didn't even know the definition of the word!

Out of curiosity, I looked up the definition: "CONCEITED—to have an exaggerated opinion of oneself, one's merits, etc." Wow, that pushes all my buttons about not wanting to be wrong! What if I claim to the world that I am great, wonderful, and brilliant and then am shot down and proven wrong? How horrifying! Perhaps I had better judge myself by a standard so much higher than anyone else's that I can never again be accused of being conceited! **NOT**!

I pay huge prices for this "twisted" state of mind. **Imagine the amount of precious life force energy that gets depleted as**

I constantly impose pressure on myself to do more! What is even sadder, is how much I deprive myself of the pleasure of living each day appreciating all that I do. I remember denying myself the pleasure of moving into my new home. When people commented on how much I must love my new place, I would think to myself, Yeah, if I ever get unpacked! (Almost a year later, I am still not completely unpacked, so I haven't yet allowed myself the full joy of my new home!)

My sense of self-worth erodes every time I deny what I have achieved. If it is true that what I am grateful for grows (and I believe this to be true), by denying my gifts, I am stunting their growth and expression. How different would my life be if I acknowledged all that I did well, was proud of who I am, and was satisfied with doing my best each day (and my best included failing and taking time to play)?

I think modesty is highly overrated in our culture. It causes us to diminish our accomplishments and dishonor our gifts. I know I certainly have done both. I am not yet comfortable singing my own praises and savoring the joy and satisfaction of what I do each day. I am reminded of a quote we should all remember:

> "Our deepest fear is not that we are inadequate. Our deepest fear is that we are powerful beyond measure. It is our light, not our darkness, that most frightens us. We ask ourselves, 'Who am I to be brilliant, gorgeous, talented and fabulous?' Actually, who are you not to be? You are a child of God. Your playing small doesn't serve the world. There's nothing enlightened about shrinking so that other people won't feel insecure around you. We were born to make manifest the glory of God that is within us. It's not just in

some of us. It's in everyone. And as we let our own light shine, we unconsciously give other people permission to do the same. As we are liberated from our own fear, our presence automatically liberates others."

Marianne Williamson, 1993

I need to focus on my light, rather than what I perceive to be my inadequacies. It seems ironic (here I go with the self-judgement, again) that in Second Degree I talk about how unlimited Reiki is and what it can do, and yet I have spent so much of my time focused on my limitations! As I allow myself the joy and satisfaction of focusing on all the great things each day, I look forward to going to sleep each night with a feeling of satisfaction, knowing that what I do and who I am is not only enough, but magnificent.

Seeking Approval

Speaking of magnificent people, as I was thinking about those I admire and aspire to be more like, I realized that they all had a certain quality, a quiet confidence that I admired. One of these people is Maya Angelou, author and poet. As I watched an interview of her one day I realized what it was that gave her this "humble confidence" and inner peace. She truly did not care what others thought of her.

In my early teens I remember being devastated at the thought of even one person not liking me. My whole identity and self-worth were dictated by being accepted. This was a very painful period in my life, as I was overweight and therefore "unacceptable" in appearance by my peers.

I desperately overcompensated for my perceived inadequacies by doing everything I thought would make others like me. This included smoking, cutting classes, and many other things I would rather not mention. The saddest part was that my self-esteem didn't seem to improve, no matter what I tried to do to fit in. I eventually learned and accepted that there would always be people who didn't like or approve of me, and that I was still "likable" without their approval. (I find it interesting that around the time in my life when I began to meditate regularly was when I stopped seeking others' approval so completely.)

I remember reading about the concept of being "internally referenced," when a person seeks approval internally rather than externally. I needed to approve of myself, not anyone else. I liked the concept and I have made progress, since now I am usually not upset if someone takes a dislike to me. I did have a little trouble not caring what someone I admired thought of me, though. I have even become quite comfortable looking silly in front of others and being able to simply enjoy myself. I saw a book a few years ago with a great title: *What you think of Me Is None of My Business*, by Terry Cole Whittaker.

In my quest to become more internally referenced, I have made fair progress. As far as appearance goes, I am much less concerned about what others think of how I dress or what my body looks like. My love of the ocean really helped: I loved being at the beach too much to worry about what others thought of how I looked in a bathing suit!

Now I have reached a more difficult phase in my growth towards "Self Approval" I have discovered that it is often harder to please myself than others. Most people consider me to be a very honest person; however, I know all the times I let a little white lie slip or I didn't tell someone the whole truth. Most people consider me a person of my word and very reliable. I will keep my word to others, as I am not willing to be known as someone who does not keep her word, but I often break promises to myself. Obviously that behavior shows that I am seeking other's approval more than my own.

I think the key I have been missing to being able to win my own approval is forgiveness. I don't expect others to be perfect in order to receive my love and respect, so why do I expect myself to be perfect before I am worthy of my own love and respect? As Spock (from *Star Trek*) would say, "That is not logical!"

To forgive myself, I need to remember that I may not always make the best choices in each moment of my life, but I did the best I could in that moment, given all of the circumstances, including my imperfections. When I forgive myself as easily as I forgive others I will be well on my way.

To be really honest: when I receive a compliment or admiration from someone, especially someone I respect and admire, I get a nice, warm inner glow . . . I feel good about me! Guess what? I wouldn't feel that good unless their recognition validated my sense of self-worth! If I was truly internally referenced and didn't feel the need to seek other's approval, I would appreciate a compliment—but it wouldn't affect how I felt about myself.

I look forward to the time when I live up to my own standards of integrity and honesty, when I am able to lovingly forgive myself if I am not perfect, and when I can laugh at myself regularly and not need external validation... Perhaps tomorrow?

self-judgement

six

TIME

I am blessed with more flexibility of time since I am self-employed. This is a mixed blessing. I have the freedom to plan my own schedule, take vacations when I want to, get up when I want to, take breaks when I want to, and even set my own deadlines. Of course there are consequences to my choices . . . usually reflected in my bank balance!

I discovered, however, that my degree of activity, or how much time I spend on work, is not always directly correlated to my income. I struggle with the self-imposed pressure that if my checking account is starving, then I need to do more or work harder. And, since my bank account never seems to have as much in it as I would like, I constantly feel I need to do more.

I have struggled with finding a balance in my life between work and play, fun and productivity. There seems to be a lot more involved than simply planning a schedule and sticking to it.

A Joyful Life

So often I get caught up in the day-to-day tasks of life: the laundry, paying bills, writing my newsletter—that I forget to make time for FUN! I have frequently decided that I will feel better when I get a lot of tasks completed, instead of spending the afternoon at the beach. I have suffered pangs of guilt when I spent half a day on the phone with girlfriends, instead of accomplishing something more productive.

I still catch myself judging the success of my day by how much I accomplished. Did I get all the tasks done on my list? Did I meet all of my deadlines (mostly self-imposed), etc.? I will look at my day and ask myself, What did I accomplish? Did I keep the monster called "running out of time" at bay?

What I seem to forget to evaluate are things like: Was I a good friend today? Did I touch someone's life in a positive way? Did I laugh today? Did I make someone smile? Did I strengthen my relationships? Did I learn something new? Did I have fun?

I once did a wonderful and revealing exercise where I was asked to imagine that I was 90 years old and had to write a brief description about my life. Did I want to write that I lived a highly productive life? That I had a clean house and made all of my deadlines? NO!

I want to be able to write about the wonderful people in my life; the warm, rich, memories; the laughter shared with friends and family; and yes, maybe about some of my accomplishments, but even those would be about the number of people I taught Reiki to or the great lectures I gave or the books I wrote.

I want to judge the success of my life by how much love and joy I was able to create, by the number of people I touched, and how much fun I had. To do this, I must make *this* the criteria for judging each day. Because my life is made up of each single day, lived one after the other.

How differently would you look at your life if you judged it by how much fun you had? Which priorities would you change? How would you greet each day?

Just some food for thought . . .

Doing and Being

I have discovered that the more I work with life force energy, the more I notice that it is my thoughts rather than my actions that affect the results in my life. It used to be that whenever things were not working out the way I wanted them to, I would ask myself, What do I need to DO differently? For example, in sales I usually needed to call on more prospective clients or present the product in a different way.

Teaching Reiki has been an amazing learning experience. I have found that my actions are not as important as my thoughts, my attitude or "beingness".

In my work I have many opportunities to see how my "being-ness" affects my results. My income is dependent on the tuition I receive from students in my classes. There are months when my classes are smaller than what I had anticipated and therefore my income was not what I had expected. Initially, I experienced fear about not being able to meet my financial obligations. So I asked myself, "What do I need to DO differently?" I decided that I hadn't worked hard enough. I needed to call more people, send out flyers; basically DO more. **The interesting thing was, the more I DID, the less students I had.**

I finally realized what had happened. My focus towards my students had shifted: instead of focusing on how I could best serve my students' needs, I had shifted to focusing on how my students could serve me.

I realized that it was my BEING that needed to shift, not my DOING!

Once I stopped my panic and focused on how grateful I am to be able to do what I love, on how rewarding it is to see the growth and changes that occur when someone takes Reiki, and how much of an honor it is to be able to do the Reiki initiations for someone, I found that I would "miraculously" connect with the students who were ready to take Reiki.

I know that both *doing* and *being* are important for success. It seems like *doing* is the masculine aspect and *being* is the feminine aspect; but balance between the two is important. Reiki energy always moves us toward greater balance and harmony and it has taught me to strive for balance to create my success.

What works for me, is to first focus on how I am BEING, and then my action, or my DOING, becomes effortless and more effective.

Effective or Efficient?

I have been told that to increase balance within myself I could change my pace and style of doing things, such as working, eating, etc.

I decided that although Reiki helps eliminate imbalances, it would be wise to prevent them altogether. It was recommended that I put my full attention on one activity at a time and complete that task before beginning the next. It sounded simple to me, so I began the next day. I immediately noticed how difficult (and boring) it seemed to eat my breakfast without reading something, or talking on the phone, or planning my day or . . .

I was told to simply put my attention on my food and eat it SLOWLY, to taste it, and to notice the different textures, etc. It was also hard to slow down when I was hungry. I admitted that this new style was a more challenging than I had originally thought.

The phone rang and my day was off to its usual start. A few hours later I stopped what I was doing and caught myself in my usual routine: at that moment I had a load of clothes in the washer, some bread baking in the oven, the dishwasher running, half of the bathroom clean (the other half was soaking), I was printing some letters on the computer, and dialing the phone. Obviously I was NOT focused on doing one task at a time!

I then realized how inefficient it would be to do only one thing at a time and how good I was at filling every moment with as much activity as possible. But, I wondered, "How important is efficiency?" Is it perhaps a reflection of a belief that there is not enough time? Do I not believe in an abundance of all things in nature? At what price am I getting so many things done quickly?

I thought of people I knew and admired who were able to ignore a ringing phone and stay totally engrossed in a conversation with someone or focused on the project at hand. I know how good it feels when I am "in the zone" or on a roll when I am writing or teaching Reiki. I know at those moments my full being, both my intellect and intuition, is centered on what I am doing.

I decided that I have valued efficiency more than the quality of my activity, and I am practicing being totally present in whatever I am doing. I am beginning to see the value in this new pace of life.

Who cares if my laundry is done today or tomorrow? Obviously, I am not going to throw some clothes in the washer and then sit and watch them be cleaned, but I don't need to sacrifice my every moment for the sake of being one day ahead in my weekly tasks. I can have less unrealistic expectations of what I will complete in a week.

And maybe, if what I am beginning to notice is true, I will get more accomplished by being totally present. I'll be more *effective* rather than more *efficient.*

t
i
m
e

I believe that by slowing down and being more focused in the present moment, my enjoyment of life and my effectiveness far outweigh the benefit of efficiency.

Honoring My Feminine Self

I am very proud of the fact that I can be described as responsible, reliable, efficient, decisive, productive, and intelligent. These qualities, however, are the strengths of my masculine energy—they are also the qualities that our culture tends to value.

My feminine side is my playful, emotional, passionate, accepting, intuitive, creative, imaginative, and perceptive energy. This is the part of me that doesn't get equal time. In fact, I often think of time as something to spend, something to use productively, something to treat as a rare and valuable commodity. If I am efficient, I am using my time well. If I were to sit on the beach and watch the waves for an hour (or more), or talk with a friend about a movie I saw, or read a novel, or play solitaire on the computer for an hour, I would typically judge this as wasting time, or indulging myself, or taking a break. I would have a hard time accepting that this use of time was valuable—from society's perspective, anyhow.

I realized how unbalanced this perspective was; that it perpetuates a feeling of scarcity and lack in my life. I often feel that

I don't have enough time, that it is out of my control, and it is something I have to spend carefully and wisely. What if I viewed time as something I *experience*, rather than something I use? What if I viewed my world from the perspective that everything unfolds in **PERFECT TIME**, and all I need to do is watch and listen for my cues and play my part in the dance of life? If I am so busy rewriting the script and trying to control the flow of time, perhaps I miss my cues altogether.

I decided to take one day a week and not schedule ANY-THING. I don't even have to get out of bed if I don't want to. It is a day to follow my whims. Do I want to go to the beach, go scuba diving, curl up with a book, chat on the Internet, watch a movie, have lunch with a friend, visit a museum, or take a child to the park? At first, I labeled this as my day to indulge myself . . . my day off. ("Off" of what? I love my work and as I am self-employed, my work and personal life are intermingled.) I guess it was a day off from productivity (Wasn't there something in the Bible about a day of rest?).

Even the words I use to describe this day (i.e. "day off") are a reflection of the way I more highly valued my masculine self. Instead, I now refer to it as my SACRED DAY. This is my day each week where I HONOR my feminine self . . . by allowing myself pleasure and the time and space to listen to my inner whims. I want to be guided by these inner whims, instead of my outer "shoulds." To simply BE instead of DOING something. I want to remember that this day is valuable. It nurtures the feminine side of me, and I believe that as I nurture this feminine side of me I will blossom in new ways . . . ways that I have never given myself the space to develop, since I have always been so diligent about being productive and making good use of my time.

Over the last couple of weeks, I have found it difficult to honor and enjoy my Sacred Day. All of the unfinished tasks, deadlines, and my feelings of a shortage of time were screaming at me while I tried to listen to what my inner self was guiding me to do (See, there I go again, thinking I have to DO something!). What I believe will happen, as I honor my feminine self and become more attuned to my inner wisdom, is that my life will flow . . . so I can actually do less and accomplish more, by listening to my inner cues.

If I **EXPERIENCE** time rather than **USE** it, could it become something that stretches and flows instead of something that gets used up and disappears? I will just have to wait, simply **BE**, and see.

t
i
m
e

seven

BEING PRESENT

This is the final section of the book, as it seems to be a thread that runs through most of the other issues I have addressed. Being present—being aware, paying attention to the moment I am experiencing—is often the solution or means to cope with whatever challenges me.

I am not being present when I am focused on self-judgement, when I am feeling rushed, or especially when I avoid uncomfortable feelings.

If I were to live even a few minutes more each day, being fully present in the moment, how much richer would my life be?

Eckhart Tolle, in his book The Power of Now, *convincingly presents that in the Now, the present moment, problems do not exist; we are complete and perfect. That's where I want to be.*

The Present Moment

The present moment is all there is. I have been coming across this concept for years. We have all heard the phrase "Be Here Now" and know that it is best to be "in the present." I have come to realize not only how valuable this is, but also how difficult it can be.

Children are the best teachers of this. (When did we lose it?) When a young child looks at an insect, nothing else exists but that insect, and she really SEES that insect! And when a child is hungry, he is HUNGRY and there is nothing else, either!

Children are said to be very observant, sometimes embarrassingly so! I think it is simply that they are more PRESENT, so they notice much more. How much am I missing in life by not being present?

Deepak Chopra, in his book *The Seven Spiritual Laws of Success*, notes that when we are in our *Dharma*, expressing our purpose in life and using our unique talent, we move into a timeless awareness. We are so immersed and fulfilled in what we are doing, we become timeless!

I realized that one of the reasons my Reiki classes are so

pleasurable for me, and I seem to have no problem holding people's attention for hours, is that when I am teaching a Reiki class, I am totally present. Nothing exists outside of the people in the room while we are in class. It makes teaching effortless and **timeless.**

When we make love, are we not (I hope) immersed in the present moment? Imagine what life would be like if we were that present in *all* that we do.

When someone listens to me and is *totally present*, I feel I am important to them, as if nothing exists in that moment but what I am saying. I am getting much better at listening that way, too!

In *The Miracle of Mindfulness*, Thich Nhat Hanh describes how we can find deep spiritual peace through the practice of Mindfulness, of which its basis is being present.

Dr. Stephan Rechtschaffen, in his wonderful book, *Time Shifting*, explains how we can expand and stretch time by becoming totally present. He also shows how profoundly healing being present can be: "When we slow down enough to be **here**, where we can act, rather than react . . . and stay in our present emotion, then and only then, will we be able to break old patterns and form a new self." POWERFUL!

Eating is a great exercise in becoming present. I had no idea how difficult it is to be totally present when eating. If I am with someone, I usually pay more attention to them than what I am eating. If I am alone, I immediately reach for something to read, or I will find myself looking out the window and realize I haven't noticed the last few bites.

When I am present while I eat (closing my eyes while chew-

being present

ing helps), the food tastes SO different. There are textures, nuances in flavors, and even temperature differences I never noticed. The biggest change is how quickly I feel full. In my 30 years of dieting, I have heard over and over again to do nothing else while eating, to eat slowly and to savor each mouthful. Why haven't I done it?

During my experiment of being present while eating, I discovered something amazing: not only did I feel full with less food, it also took HOURS longer than usual to get hungry again! I believe that when we put attention on our food, we enliven the energy of the food and it nourishes us even more on an energetic and cellular level. Our life force energy flows to everything else we put our attention on, therefore it stands to reason that it would affect our food, also.

Deepak Chopra also states that one of the key factors of success is being in the present moment. "When action is performed in present-moment awareness, it is most effective . . . as long as your attention is in the present, then your intent for the future will manifest, because the future is created in the present."

I have lots of motivation to keep in the present moment: my desires will be fulfilled, eating my meals takes on the sensuality of making love, I can heal old patterns, and I can even shift time! Beyond all of that, my life takes on new depth, richness, and a deeper sense of timeless being.

Embracing Pain

At a Reiki gathering in 1995, Phyllis Lei Furumoto, Lineage Bearer of Usui Shiki Ryoho, spoke about pain: "My relationship with pain has come from a place of wanting it to go away and avoiding it at all costs, to allowing it to be an ally. To be something that guides me and leads me and gets my attention, so I'll do something. I also realize that there are many different levels and kinds of pain and there's no way to compare it or analyze it. It just is so."

When I heard this, I realized how I come from that place of wanting it to go away and avoiding it at all costs. I often use Reiki for my physical pain: headaches, menstrual cramps, etc. I also avoid the precursor to pain—discomfort—by distracting myself with food or some other activity. I seem to not be willing to accept pain or discomfort.

I recently had a detoxifying experience that was very painful: a pounding headache, a very sore throat, nausea, and vomiting. I couldn't take any pain medication because I couldn't keep anything in my stomach. As I used Reiki to help with the pain, with only temporary success, I realized that rather than trying to make the pain go away, maybe I just had to accept the pain and BE with it for a while.

I remember reading a comment made by a woman who had successfully stopped drinking. When she was asked if she ever craved a drink, she replied, "Yes, often. But I learned that *sometimes I just had to sit with it.*" I had never considered "just sitting with" my discomfort. I always tried to avoid it or make it go away.

As I sat with my headache and sore throat, etc., I was able to accept my pain and discomfort and embrace it as a part of the detoxification process. As long as I was running away from pain, I was not in control. I was actually fearing the pain. When I stopped running, I stopped being afraid. **It turned out that the fear of pain was worse than the pain itself.** Pain was just pain. For one moment it felt unbearable. I stayed with it, and then it eased off a little. I could handle it, feel it, and I was okay! It was very freeing to realize that I didn't have to fear pain.

I thought of a friend's experience of pain during labor. In the Bradley Method childbirth classes, she was taught to understand the transformation her body was going through, to relax, and embrace the pain of labor. She learned that she could handle the pain of each contraction, one at a time. If she looked beyond the moment and began to fear the pain of the next contraction, she would have made it much harder to bear, and may have chosen medication out of fear of future pain. I saw her embrace each pain as an ally to the birth of her child.

We learn from infancy that pain is something that needs to be fixed rather than something to experience. I found myself following this belief with my friend's two-month-old daughter. I had a difficult time allowing the baby to cry and be in discomfort with gas pain. She was fed, dry, warm, and being held; yet still crying (shrieking may describe it better). I felt inadequate because I couldn't fix it. When young children are crying, we often hear, "Don't cry." In truth, they are simply experiencing their pain. I think the hardest thing a parent must do is to stand by while their children are in pain and allow them to experience it as necessary.

I would like to learn to embrace pain as my ally; to accept it is a part of my life experience and to see if it leads me somewhere. If I fear pain, I cannot be led somewhere or understand its message. I believe the more I am able to embrace pain, the more empowered I will be in my life. I will not be running from things in fear and avoidance, but embracing each moment of my life more fully.

being present

Embracing the Future With Wonderment

I was anticipating spending Christmas with my sister's children and I realized how far from the sense of wonderment I have journeyed lately. I remember what it felt like as a child seeing a bright, sparkly Christmas tree, and the excitement and anticipation of the delight that Christmas morning would bring. It was a vivid feeling of knowing that something absolutely wonderful was about to happen. I have recognized that look on the faces of young children numerous times. Not just at Christmas, but throughout the year.

There is something magical and attractive about approaching life with wonderment.

I have a close friend who has visited me in Hawaii a few times. I experience my home with new eyes when she is here. As we walk away from the airport gate, she is exclaiming with exuberance, "Look at those flowers! Smell them! Look at the mountains! Look at that adorable child!"

I realize that I have not been seeing my home, the people around me, or the blessings in my life with wonderment. If I could experience each day of my life as if it were something new and fascinating, I could live in wonderment. (Perhaps there is a blessing if we lose our memory . . . then everything is new.)

I was talking with a friend who had discovered she was pregnant. Her initial reaction was panic. She thought of the exhaustion and struggles she had raising her first child (who was heading off to college). She saw the next 20 years of her life disappearing in front of her, as she anticipated putting her own needs and desires aside while she cared for her child. She felt burdened, angry, and scared.

Then, she went through a transformation. She realized that THIS child did not have to be a struggle like raising her first child was. *That it was only the projection of her past onto her future that brought out all of these unpleasant thoughts and feelings.* This time she had the loving support of the baby's father, the wisdom of more years (rather than the burden of her past memories), and the realization that each moment of life is a completely new and unique experience. She started to feel and talk to her new baby with a feeling of wonder . . . wondering what new and exciting things this unexpected change in her life would bring.

Albert Einstein said, "Anyone to whom this feeling is alien, who is no longer capable of wonderment and lives in a state of fear is a dead man."

After reading that quote, I realized that *fear* was the culprit. Fear has stolen my wonderment away! I realized that in childhood I *expected* great things to happen . . . why wouldn't they? I had no prior experience to tell me differently. I would see a child on the playground and run over and say "Hello," knowing I would

being present

have a new friend to play with. I did not worry about whether or not that child would like me, or whether I was pretty enough, or smart enough or how they would respond. I just expected a new friend. As a young child I did NOT project my past experiences onto the expectation of what I was about to experience.

How can I avoid projecting my past onto my future? If I am able to approach life with a sense of wonderment, how different will it be? I do believe that "To Think is To Create," that our thoughts are what manifest our reality. I believe that energy flows where my attention goes and for the majority of my day, I tended to recreate my past experiences. It is so pervasive.

If I go to a restaurant and receive poor service or a mediocre meal, every time I think about that restaurant, I assume I will have the same experience. In truth, this would be unlikely. The person who gave me poor service might have had a fight with his spouse, the chef could have improved on her food preparation, and someone new might even own or manage the restaurant. One might argue that yes, perhaps once was a fluke, but what if it happens a second time? I would counter, how much of my expectations influence what I experience the second time?

I want to set up reminders to myself throughout the day so that I ask myself, "What 'filters of the past' am I using to influence what I am now experiencing?" to wake me up to the wonderment of each moment.

Fun

I recently took a workshop that gave me several opportunities to practice being fully present. One of the many benefits I got from this workshop was a realization that I do not have enough fun or make enough mischief in my life. I recognized that my playful side is a very large part of me and it has been neglected. It is as if my fullness cannot be completely expressed without including my playfulness.

This started me thinking about what I consider to be fun. I realized that some of the things that used to be fun have disappeared from my life. I enjoy witty comments and used to use sarcasm a lot. I noticed that I don't make the same sarcastic comments I used to and when I do use sarcasm, it doesn't seem as funny anymore. I think that over the years I have felt more peaceful within, and so the hurtful, sharp edge of sarcasm has lost its appeal. I used to play practical jokes, and now find it harder to find jokes where the recipient sees the humor instead of experiencing discomfort.

I DO like to laugh at myself and am delighted when I am surprised or when the joke is on me. It takes some creativity to come up with playful ideas and jokes, especially spontaneous mischief. I have become rusty in that area and have decided to bring forth my mischievous self more often.

I asked other people what 'fun' is to them. I found that we all had different ideas of what was fun. Some found relaxing, peaceful activities, such as hiking or sailing fun; while others felt sports, movies, and fine dining were fun. I enjoy all of these things, too; yet I discovered that what really satisfied the fun part of me, which has been neglected and unexpressed, are things that really make me laugh. In other words, to me, I need to laugh to feel as though I am having fun.

I recognized that I want more laughter in my life. I mean the deep, whole-body laughter that stops time and engulfs the moment in delight. You know, those moments with friends when you laugh so hard your bellies ache, tears come to your eyes, and you can't explain what is so funny. Or the look of surprise on someone's face when they really WERE surprised at a surprise party. Or the laughter that indicates the delight that babies get when they are tossed in the air and caught or when they learn to play peek-a-boo and giggle over and over again.

I want to bring back the child-like aspect of fun and playfulness that seems to have diminished in my life. It seems to have been forgotten amidst the seriousness of life: work, families, and responsibilities to others. It is time for FUN! I can be caring, loving, and responsible and still play and create spontaneous mischief, too!

What is fun for you? What makes you laugh? When was the last time you laughed so hard there were tears in your eyes? Do you have a child-like side of yourself that hasn't appeared lately? Wanna come out and play?

Powerful Thought

In Reiki class I sometimes talk about the fact that our thoughts are energy, and yet I often seem to forget this in my day-to-day life. I constantly have thoughts "beaming" from me, without any consideration of how those thoughts affect others or myself. In the Buddhist tradition of "mindfulness," one of the practices is to be aware of what we are putting our attention on and staying in the moment. I know if I was able to consistently do this, for even a small percentage of the time, my life would be very different.

A few weeks ago I was given an unexpected gift during a casual conversation: I was eating lunch during a workshop with a young man who followed a very healthy eating regime. I knew that most of the food on my plate he would consider harmful to his health and never eat it. I remembered earlier that day, when I had walked past someone smoking and I had thought to myself, "What a disgusting habit. How can he do that to himself and pollute the air around us?" (This thought is pretty unfair, since I smoked two packs a day for many years, and know how difficult it is to quit.)

Being me, someone who typically blurts out whatever has wandered through my mind, (another reason to practice more mindfulness) I asked this young man if he had similar thoughts when he saw people eat in unhealthy ways. His reply woke me up. He said, "I used to have judgmental thoughts like that, but then I asked myself if that thought really benefited the person it was directed at. Now, when I find myself reacting to someone's choices that I wouldn't do, I simply send them a blessing with the intent that whatever they put into their body will nourish and serve them."

I was embarrassed and ashamed at my own judgmental and negative thoughts. I realized that whenever I have those kinds of thoughts, it really does harm the other person . . . even if I never say the words out loud. To bring this awareness home even more, that very afternoon at the workshop they did a demonstration using muscle testing, to show how the thoughts of not only the person being tested, but also the thoughts of those of us in the room, could impact the strength of the person being tested!

For those of you not familiar with muscle testing (also referred to as applied kinesiology), it is a process where the strength of the body can be checked (such as resisting an arm being pushed down). Whenever there is a thought, question, or a substance introduced to the person being tested, if it is not a strengthening influence, the muscle being tested will be noticeably weaker. If what is introduced has a positive influence on the person, then the muscle will be noticeably stronger.

In the demonstration that afternoon, they showed that when the person being tested thought loving thoughts, she had a lot of strength in her body; but when she thought about an unresolved conflict, she was extremely weak. In addition, they had her think a loving thought, and then asked all of us to think a negative thought about her. Even though she was thinking a loving thought, the impact of OUR thoughts weakened her body! Later on, it was demonstrated that she could counteract the effect of any negative thoughts toward her by blessing us and sending us unconditional love.

This was a great physical demonstration of how the energy of our thoughts impacts not only ourselves, but also those around us. I have become much more aware of how often I have critical or negative thoughts flitting through my mind. I really believe that "to think is to create" and I know I have a long way to go before I project strengthening thoughts most of the time.

One of the things I can do is regularly notice the quality of my thoughts. I can have things around that help me check in. I can also keep things in my environment that trigger loving thoughts. For example, when I have flowers in my home, they always bring up thoughts of appreciation, for their beauty and their scent. I have gifts from people that stir up warm memories when I see the gift. I have my collection of sea turtles, given to me by people who know my connection to them, to remind me to have a loving, positive perspective. Since I am usually more aware of my feelings than my thoughts, I can easily check in and notice how I am feeling. If I am not feeling peaceful, happy, or joyful, I can be sure that I have been generating weakening thoughts. All I need to do when I notice this is choose to think about things in a more loving way.

I believe that our thoughts affect our health and the whole world around us. If we can remember (or imagine) that every

being present

time we think something, our thought creates a vibration within ourselves, as well as sending out a wave of energy to whatever or whomever the thought is focused on. Thus it becomes very important to think wisely. It is much easier for me to forgive someone when I am aware of how damaging my unforgiving thoughts and feelings are, especially to myself! We can even take this concept further: like attracts like, and whatever we are thinking or feeling is like a magnet that attracts everything we experience in our lives.

Resonance

I said previously: ". . . like attracts like, and that whatever we are thinking or feeling is like a magnet that attracts everything we experience in our lives."

For some time now I have realized that when I react to something someone says or does, it is a reflection of something within me. This means that if I dislike it when a friend of mine makes a judgmental comment about someone, I am reacting to the part of me that is judgmental. It also means that when I really admire a quality in someone, I would not be able to recognize that quality unless I had it, too!

I want to take this idea further. I believe that everything we experience is brought about by our consciousness. That means that if my car is broken into and vandalized, or something is stolen, it is a reflection of my vibration. Now, if that occurred, I could self-righteously say to myself, "I haven't stolen or damaged someone else's property!" However, I need to ask myself, "Have I behaved in a way that didn't respect other people's property or space? Perhaps simply making noise when my neighbors wanted some peace and quiet?"

Or, more subtly, did I have thoughts of fearing my property would be damaged? When we fear something, our energy flows to that possibility (remember, energy flows where our attention goes) and we give it power.

A great analogy for this idea is a tuning fork. Tuning forks are designed to vibrate (or resonate) at a specific tone or frequency. When we strike a tuning fork tuned to the note of "C", it will vibrate at the frequency of a perfect "C" and we will hear that sound. If we hold another tuning fork near it, which is *also* tuned to the note of "C," the second fork will vibrate and 'sing' the note of "C" without being struck! I am told it will affect another same-tone tuning fork even as far away as the length of a football field. The interesting thing is that this spontaneous vibration occurs ONLY if both forks are tuned to the same note. You could hold up forks of different notes and nothing will happen.

Do you see the analogy? If we RESONATE with a certain vibration, it will "vibrate" in our lives. If we don't, then it doesn't happen. A spiritual teacher once pointed out that even Gandhi resonated with some degree of violence, or he wouldn't have died a violent death. When I mentioned this to someone recently, she pointed out to me that Gandhi *did* indeed display violence— to himself and his body with his hunger strikes. Subtle, huh!

If I accept this concept, how do I change my resonance? If I look at my current life, things are really good in most areas, but I frequently experience a lack of time. I need to look at where my thoughts and feelings vibrate with "lack." I do notice that I get into a mindset where I feel rushed and short of time. I can plan my day and my commitments less tightly and I can stay aware of my thoughts and catch myself thinking about lack.

I often catch myself going over all the things I need to take care of and make myself feel overwhelmed, instead of *only* focusing on what I need to handle today. How many times each day do I tell myself "hurry up!" or "I'm running out of time?" If I catch the thought right away, I can simply choose to look at the situation differently. I can remind myself that everything flows in perfect time. The more I stay focused on the immediate moment and what I am doing, the more abundant time feels.

My challenge to myself is to be more aware of my thoughts and feelings and to stay more present in each moment. We will see how abundantly my life unfolds as I culture more time and a peaceful pace in my life.

What do you want different in your life? Can you change your own "resonance" about it? I know we are on the threshold of great change . . . I can feel the vibration.

being present

Conclusion

Now that I have reviewed the past seven years of introspection I don't know if I should be wearing a halo or a dunce cap!

In some ways I have made progress, yet I still find myself doing things that make me crazy and make my life more difficult and less conscious.

In truth, I have made several circuits on this spiraling journey and I can look back and see there is more depth in my life. I am more conscious and aware than I was seven years ago. I judge myself less often and less harshly. I am more honest and accepting. I like myself better and am at peace more often. I even have fun and laugh once in a while!

It has been good for me to write this book, to be vulnerable and share my thoughts with you. I hope they have touched you in various ways ... made you laugh, cry, and wonder and question your life. I hope you had moments when you could see yourself and realized that most of us go through similar experiences and that you are not alone. At the very least, I hope you were entertained.

Conclusion

My journey doesn't end here. I am not sure I have an ulti-mate destination, simply that with each step and each word, I am becoming more authentic and more fully who I am capable of becoming.

I will continue writing and I will make these thoughts and experiences available to you as I continue on my naked journey.

(Visit my website, http://www.MyNakedJourney.com for future chapters and to share some of your own stories.)

Bibliography

Chicken Soup for the Soul: 101 Stories to Open the Heart and Rekindle the Spirit. Jack Canfield and Mark Victor Hansen, eds. Health Communications, Incorporated, Deerfield, FL, 1994. (As well as the dozens of other books in this series.)

Eating in the Light of the Moon: How Women Can Transform Their Relationships with Food through Myths, Metaphors, and Storytelling. Anita A. Johnston, Ph.D., Gurze Books, Carlsbad, CA, 2000.

Fire In The Soul: A New Psychology of Spiritual Optimism. Joan Borysenko, Ph.D., Warner Books, Incorporated, New York, NY, 1994.

Illusions: The Adventures of A Reluctant Messiah. Richard Bach. Dell Publishing Incorporated, New York, NY, 1979.

The Miracle of Mindfulness: A Manual on Meditation. Thich Nhat Hanh, Mobi Ho (Translator), Beacon Press, Boston, MA, 1996.

The Power of Now: A Guide to Spiritual Enlightenment. Eckhart Tolle. New World Library, Novato, CA, 1999.

Bibliography

The Seven Spiritual Laws of Success: A Practical Guide to the Fulfillment of Your Dreams. Deepak Chopra. Amber-Allen Publishing, San Rafael, CA, 1995.

Time Shifting: Creating More Time to Enjoy Your Life. Stephan Rechtschaffen, Doubleday, Westminster MD 1997.

Walking in a Crowd of Angels: A Collection, Volume 1. Beth Terry. Lezard Press, Honolulu, HI, 1999.

What You Think of Me Is None of My Business. Terry Cole-Whittaker. Berkley Publishing Group, East Rutherford, NJ, 1988.

On Reiki

Traditionally, Reiki has been taught as an oral tradition, where a student spends time with a Reiki Master. Many of us still teach Reiki in this manner, as I do. Today there are countless different books, web sites and even videos on Reiki, presenting a wide range of perspectives about this healing art.

I believe that Reiki has been a guiding force in my personal journey, and that the system of Reiki that I follow, The Usui Shiki Ryoho System, provided me with a depth of experience that some other approaches would not have.

The resources on Reiki that I have listed below are ones that I personally recommend. If you are drawn to Reiki, I wish you a deep and fulfilling journey.

BOOKS

Reiki: Hawayo Takata's Story. Helen J. Haberly, Archedigm, Incorporated, Olney, MD, 1990.

Living Reiki: Takata's Teachings. Takata, as told to Fran Brown. LifeRhythm, 1992.

MAGAZINES

Reiki Magazine International. Holmmij vof, Publisher. Amsterdam, Netherlands. www.ReikiMagazine.com
U.S. contact: Paul Haines & Upasana Grugen, P.O. Box 5614, Eugene, OR 97405. (541) 686-8378, upasana@rampaenterprises.com

WEB SITES

www.usuireiki.com
The Usui System of Reiki Healing, Usui Shiki Ryoho. This site provides information for anyone interested in Reiki, including students and teachers of this healing art.

www.reikitreatments.com
REIKITREATMENTS.COM™ is an informational referral service for a global community of Reiki providers—Reiki Masters and Reiki Practitioners—who practice the Usui System of Reiki Healing. Reiki providers who are registered with the service assert that they meet certain REIKITREATMENTS.COM™ self-assessment guidelines and agree in writing to abide by the REIKITREATMENTS.COM(tm) code of ethics.

www.reikialliance.com
The Reiki Alliance is an international community of Reiki Masters of the Usui System of Reiki Healing—Usui Shiki Ryoho. We teach and practice the Usui System of Reiki by maintaining the time-honored form passed through the direct spiritual lineage of Mikao Usui, Chujiro Hayashi, Hawayo Takata, and Phyllis Lei Furumoto.

After meeting in 1982, a group of masters gathered the following year in British Columbia, Canada to create The Reiki Alliance and acknowledge Takata's granddaughter, Phyllis Lei Furumoto, as her successor.

Since 1983 The Reiki Alliance has met annually to explore the path of mastery. We have grown from twenty members at our founding meeting to a current membership of more than 700 representing forty-five countries.

The mission of The Reiki Alliance is to honor and practice Reiki, acknowledge the spiritual lineage, support one another and deepen our experience as masters and teachers, and help steward the Usui System of Reiki Healing.

o
n

r
e
i
k
i

About the Author

Maureen O'Shaughnessy was born and raised on Vancouver Island in British Columbia, Canada. She has lived in Hawaii since 1979 and is a graduate of the University of Hawaii.

She began her work with Reiki in 1991, and completed her training in 1995 with Reiki Master Jessica Osborn-Turner. She teaches Reiki full time, traveling between Hawaii, the mainland U.S. and Canada. She teaches classes regularly in Honolulu, has been a guest speaker for many organizations, and has appeared on numerous radio and TV shows.

For more information go to: www.reiki-hawaii.com or www.mynakedjourney.com

Order Information

Call Toll Free: **866-729-3636**

On-line: **www.MyNakedJourney.com**

Fax this form to: **866-782-3622**

Mail this form to:

Pua'ena Publishing
150 Hamakua Dr., PMB 732
Kailua, HI 96734

My Naked Journey: A Reiki Master's Quest to Live an Authentic Life

Please send _____ copies @ $14.95 (tax included) _____

plus S/H $3.50 for first book ($2 each add'l book)   _____

Total enclosed _____

Name _____

Address _____

City _____ State _____ Zip _____

Phone (____)_____ e-mail _____

Payment:

_____ Check or money order *(payable to Maureen O'Shaughnessy)*

_____ Visa _____ Mastercard

Card number _____

Expiration _____ Name on card _____

Billing address_____

Signature _____

Thank you for your order!

http://www.MyNakedJourney.com